DENNIS SHRUBSHAL
in the East End of I
child in a family of s
through the WW2 y
School until 1948.

Dennis started work as a Railway clerk in London and then went into the RAF in 1952 as a Radar Operator for 2 years. Since then he has spent 54 years in the Building Trade as a Master Builder. He married in 1957 and has two daughters and five grandchildren. He played bowls for 38 years including representing Essex over 100 times.

Dennis first wrote poetry in 1973 but more prolifically in the last five years with the advent of a word processor. Now semi-retired, he lives in the house he built 40 years ago in Benfleet, Essex.

Dennis Shrubshall is now known as "Shrubby the Essex Bard".

Published in paperback by Silverwood Books 2009
www.silverwoodbooks.co.uk

ISBN 978-1-906236-14-4

British Library Cataloguing in Publication Data
A CIP catalogue record for this book is available from the British Library

Set in 11pt Bembo by SilverWood Books
Printed and bound in Great Britain by
CPI Antony Rowe, Chippenham and Eastbourne

A Tapestry of Verse

by

DENNIS SHRUBSHALL

SilverWood

This Volume is dedicated to my wife
Doris Marjorie Shrubshall
more affectionately known as "Terry"
for her continued support in my writing
and her contribution of the tapestries
displayed on the cover of this book

Contents

Foreword

A Tapestry of Verse by Dennis Shrubshall is a remarkable collection of poetry and verse, which eloquently speaks of the author's journey through life in a way which connects to one's own very personal experiences.

As someone who has experienced at first hand the expectation and reality of conflict *The British Soldier,* for example, is a beautifully simple and emotional reminder of the discordant journey one takes as a soldier; the realities of conflict stripped bare and the truth that all soldiers irrespective of country, cause or race eventually dream of just going home.

Giles Penfound
Documentary Photographer
gilespenfound.com

Part One

Life's Tapestries

*A general selection of varied subjects
depicted in meaningful rhyme*

WRITING TODAY

Poems and Odes are more popular today
Than ever they've been in the past
'cos with your friendly computer for company
You can write down your thoughts really fast
Not like the days on the paper you'd scrawl
With a handy pencil or pen
And then get out your Erasor
And start all over again
It's easier to write and edit, if you must
There is much more time to think
Of a stimulating subject
That will take you to the brink
Of that vast vocabulary of words
Ever constant on your mind
Eager to spill out on to the screen
When a suitable subject you find
And you don't have to come to a conclusion
But "save as" till the next time you write
Whether today or tomorrow
Or even next Saturday night
Where in the interim period
The subject in your mind you will muse
On how your poem you will finish
What final line will you use
For the Start and Finale are important
Whether you joke or taunt, sometimes tease
The ultimate aim of a writer
To hope their compositions will please
Those who find reading a pleasure
Scanning Poems and Odes in rhyme
And if a line or a verse brings a smile to a face
It's worth writing perhaps one more time.

21st June 2008

Rambling

Oh! how I long for the countryside
For solitude and peace
A place of pleasant sanctuary
Where worries seem to cease
For here I can bare my very soul
In perfect dignity
Away from all of the strangers
And the only critic is me
I stroll along the country lanes
Until a style I see
A place for entry to the fields beyond
In the world where I long to be
Far away from the towns and cities
The traffic, the hustle, the noise
Here is my Utopia
Where we used to play as boys
Looking out across the hills
When the Sun is' coming to rest
Displaying a carpet of green and gold
Before the Twilight that I love best
There's oats & barley & maize and wheat
For Harvest time is here
The time when labourers work from dawn to dusk
To make sure the fields are clear
Then straightaway out with the Tractor and Plough
And till the land for next year
As I'm wandering now past the Farm House
I'm invited in by the Farmer and his Wife
To join them for Supper and a glass of Cider
It's a custom in country life

When I take my leave and stroll along
In the last of the daylight hours
I hear the birds in evening song
As surroundings my eyes scours
I see the run of the wily Fox
The hoot of the Barn Owl from a tree
It seems as though they are putting on a show
Especially for me
And that's why I walk my solitary path
The animals are my company.

2nd September 2008

A WINTRY DAY

At the window I stand and stare
The clouds go drifting by
As I look to the far horizon
In an ever darkening sky
Where the sun has left just a tinge of gold
From a day that has come to it's end
Without the sight of a rainbow
Though rain it did descend
But sunshine found a time to glow
When hope was nearly gone
Of a break in the squally showers
That forever carried on
Throughout the morn and afternoon
Torrential rain then gaps
Which helped to build our hopes
Of sunshine again perhaps
Will tomorrow bring the wind of change
Or shall we see more rain
Is there hope of a break in sight
Are we still in the doldrums again
Forecasts I don't understand
'tho the Weatherman seems to know
It's all about pressures and Isobars
The "Telly" told me so
And now a new day is dawning
As I look to a lightening sky
'tis said hope springs eternal

The clouds fly fast and high
Which might bring about a change
To the ever constant flow
From the heavens up above us and
Flood this land below
I think I can see some blue in the sky
Clouds they are quick to fade
And disappear in the distance
A beautiful morn' is displayed
Prayers are now answered
To all of us here below
As a steady stream of Sunbeams
Set a welcome Golden glow.

8th February 2007

Hingham

The morning's welcomes another new day
The Sun is shining brightly
To Norfolk now I'm on my way
The route may vary slightly
But first I must travel a good few miles
Through Essex to reach the border
Of the neighbouring County of Cambridgeshire
I saw the hills as I came toward her
And as I came to Duxford
A decision I had to make
Shall I carry on up the Motorway
Or is it the sliproad I should take
And make my way to Newmarket
Through the villages on the way
And on to Mildenhall, Thetford and Watton
'cos I've got a game of Bowls to play
With just a few more townships
Before my final destination
Will the lovely village of Hingham
Live up to its reputation?

I've passed Watton Green and Scoulton
And appearing on the scene
Is the beautiful old Parish Church
Right next to the Bowling Green
On the left hand side just past the church
The Local Inn is found
To satisfy our lust for food
And a couple of pints we've "downed
Back up the road the village shops
Selling Souvenirs and Corn Dollies
And on this particular sunny day
Quite a lot of Ice Lollies
A really pleasant day was spent
Hospitality hard to beat
Then travel home through Attleborough and Diss
To make my visit to Norfolk complete.

27th May 2007

THE OLD SHOP

I take a walk to yesteryear
To see what I can find
What resourceful relic of the past
Has someone left behind
While walking down the country lane
There in front of me
Is this old fashioned brick building
Waiting for me to see
What treasures might I soon find
Forgotten memories unearth
Perhaps some National Heritage
Beyond monetary worth
The ancient ledge and braced stable-door
Fallen into dis-repair
And I walked beneath the arched head frame
To see what was hidden there
Various signs adorned the walls
Now with rust and dirt on top
Indicative that this quaint building
May have housed the Village shop
Where villagers may have purchased
Venus Soap or a pair of Frisby's Boots
For there were no Supermarkets then
Only this shop with local recruits
To man the tills and fill the shelves
And cater for what customers require
As they wander round selecting goods
Or just warm by the open fire

On the shelves there were glass stoppered jars
With sweets and biscuits inside
And a tug of the hand from the children
Expectant with eyes open wide
Or did Mum want some disinfectant
A loaf of bread and some butter and cheese
Perhaps some sausages, potatoes and carrots
To make a meal for her husband to please
All of this I imagined with my eyes closed tight
After a glimpse of the surroundings there
Standing in the remnants of a bygone age
Of a time when folks used to care
Where respect and reverence were an everyday occurrence
Sadly missing in my mind I must say
As I stepped once more into the daylight
After my trip to a long gone yesterday.

28th September 2008

CONTENTMENT

If the simple life is the one you choose
You've lots to gain and little to lose
For monetary gain doesn't measure wealth
It's sometime's measured in happiness and health
And with these two assets, you'll little need
Ill gotten gains of those with greed
Who by devious actions will only succeed
To bring about their own demise
When the healthy and happy can capitalise
And live in a world of contentment.

25th June 2007

An Image In Rhyme

She was sitting there upon the screen
There was something in her eyes
Was it a hint of sadness
I'm trying hard to visualise
The personality behind the smile
How was she treated by the world
In which she lived her lonely life
Waiting for magic to be unfurled
Like a flag that's left to lie too long
It's message under wraps
Until it's hoisted up aloft
In full view and then perhaps
This Lady's once again rekindled
The flame that once shone so bright
As life has offered a second chance
In order that she just might
Return and use the talent
In those fingers and mind so young
To create once again those pieces of art
Which her Dad's praises had sung
For it seems that her strength overcame demons
That recently blighted her life
And no doubt the love of her Children helped
To resolve all her personal strife
And to enable her to continue to write, and paint
In tranquillity and ease
Creating masterpieces so that others she might please.

6th September 2007

East Anglian LNER

We're sitting in a railway compartment
At a London Mainline Station
Waiting for our journey to start
Full of anticipation
And as through the windows
We glance now & again
We see folks passing with luggage
And boarding the train
There's hustle and bustle
With barrows and Porters
All making sure the luggage
Is in the right quarters
In the time honoured Guards Van
Full to capacity, taking the strain
Of the ten carriages coupled
To make up the Train
The locomotive's been coupled
And building up steam
So that once on the way
We reach speeds extreme
Especially with this "loco"
"The East Anglian" we've seen
Easily recognised
With it's livery of green
The Porters are standing back now
The whistle the Guard has blown
And soon we'll be speeding down the track
In a dreamworld of our own
Slowly we pass the City suburbs
Gradually increasing speed.

But it's not until we're into the country
The limits he'll try to exceed
With the throttle back and the whistle loud
Steam is hissing
Smoke's like a cloud
As it passes our windows
Like a funeral shroud
Eager to ever increase the pace
As tho' the journey to Norwich
Was a dramatic race
To conquer the distance
In the shortest time
Stopwatch in hand
The driver's sublime
But in the excitement
Ipswich we'd long passed
Without even noticing
We were going so fast
With a last blast on the whistle
As we rounded the bend
Our magic journey to Norwich
Had come to an end
But the thoughts and the Memories
Although they may fade
Will stay in our minds
For many a decade.

7th December 2007

A Shopping Spree

I went out shopping on Saturday
To see what I could find
'cos I've got a more than ample chest
And an oversize behind
I went in Marks & Spencer's
In Littlewood's as well
It wasn't going to be my lucky day
As I could quickly tell
I looked at Bra's & Lingerie
At jumpers and gear for sports
But how am I going to interest men
Wearing Khaki "Dad's Army" shorts
I asked the girl about mini skirts
She replied "with no offence meant"
Why not go to Camping and General
And see if they've got a small tent
But now she'd got my dander up
I'm ready for the fight
So I bought a two-piece suit, with baggy trousers
To wear on Saturday night
In order to write a rhyme like this
Although it's only a tease
I'm going to sign off with my pseudonym
Dorothy Violet Louise.

Written through the eyes of a woman for a dare.
6th June 2007

ALL SAFE AND SECURE

When all the world is fast asleep
My world comes to waking
Thinking what the night may bring
What chances will I be taking
When on Patrol I make my rounds
To check that all is well
The Locks, The Gates The Fences
My instincts warn me well
As I walk the lonely midnight hour
Hoping I won't find
Something wrongfully amiss
Or mistakenly left behind
Like a satchel, a hammer or wrench
That spells alarm to me
Has there been a break-in
Is someone hiding in the nearby vicinity
All of these thoughts go through my mind
As round the fence I walk
How long will it be before
I meet a colleague to whom I can talk
Perhaps confide in a worry
Or even get them to check with me
The reason that gives me some concern
About the security
Of the patch that I'm patrolling
For weeks night after night
Each night filled with a fervent hope
That I'll get through the night alright
The hours pass quite quickly
And the dawn is here again
So with a sigh of relief I sign off
Until duty calls again.

6th December 2007

LAW IN RETROSPECT

Thro' the eyes of a man of today
Violence seems to abound
Compared with times when as a lad
It was seldom to be found
You could walk the streets in safety
Never turn the key in the door
And children could play in freedom
But they can't do that any more
Though World War II was raging
The bombs they fell like rain
And with only a part time Police Force
The law was hard to maintain
Explosions and shrapnel were commonplace
Almost every day
Though our enemy was the Luftwaffe
And not the I.R.A.
Often I heard of Black Marketeers
Thieves, pick pockets and "Shady's"
But never once did I hear of teenagers
Mugging and raping old ladies
A dispute often settled
With an old fashioned 'scrap'
Was considered honourable and manly
Instead of today, when they gang up at dark
And creep up behind with a "Stanley"
The unwritten rule of the lawless
Was a gun or a knife not to use
To avoid the ultimate judgement
And die in the "Hangman's Noose"
But alas in today's world of affluence
"Do gooders" seem to be rife
And all they do in the end it seems
Is to cheapen the value of life.

May 1993

A Rhyme in Time

Funny words & sayings past
Very good subjects all
Giving rise to speculation
Or perhaps no thought at all
But if you sit and ponder
Words seem to come one at a time
Then put them all together maybe
You'll find that some of them rhyme
Then comes the time you must decide
Do the words say what you mean
Or is there some ambiguity
Can error by some be seen
It's similar to doing a puzzle
Where the pieces appear to be right
But having turned them every conceivable way
You while away hours at night
So if as you battle for hours with words
Which help fill your hours of leisure
You may find in time, you've created a rhyme
Which may give the less fortunate much pleasure.

DAYBREAK

On the horizon the dawn is breaking
The air is wet with morning dew
Birds their morning chorus making
In the sky a hint of blue
Suddenly the Sun appears
Clouds are tinged with gold
Now the world is slowly waking
A glorious daybreak to behold
Is it April or September
Leaves of green or gold will tell
Calendar's not necessary
Signs of nature show me well
Mushrooms sprouting, there's some clover
Down the lane the tractor's roar
Once again the night is over
A country morn is here once more
Villagers now they are appearing
Noisy vehicles the silence take
But I alone am the lucky one
To witness a tranquil DAYBREAK.

September 1994

A Mother's Role

Today as I just sit and think
Of days already past
My thoughts go back
To my childhood days
Has my Life gone by too fast
The more I try to concentrate
Events that once seemed small
Come racing back into my mind
How much can I re-call
Of days when just a little lad
Of young and tender years
To Primary School I was duly enrolled
While Mum just lingered outside the School gates
And up and down patrolled
Till her young son with other children
Disappeared inside
And when the doors were finally closed
She just broke down and cried
For this was something new to her
To leave the youngster on his own
This baby she used to sit and cuddle
To a Schoolboy now had grown
And then the years go rushing by
From Baby, to Boy then Teen
But where did all the days go
Of those years between
But Mum just did the best she could
Tho' poor she still bestowed
A lifetime of wisdom and love
To set me on Life's busy road.

.

FLOWERS

January, Frost is clinging
From trees and boughs on high
Like a shroud of white it lays
Set against a clear blue sky.
Drifting into February
Rising bulbs are seen
Snowdrops and Daffodils show their heads
Spreading colour to a carpet of green.
March winds blow their icy blast
Some of the Tulips are showing at last
Has the Winter really passed
Now that April's here.
Bringing with it frequent showers
Trees their leaves will grow
Roses looking even stronger
Their rich silk heads now show.
With May we're looking ever forward
Warm Summer days are not far away
Flowers now are in abundance
In the fields the fresh cut hay.
June, the Sun is scorching down
Parching tender grass
Will it last this lovely weather
Or just as quickly pass.
July, the Peonies in splendour
Their life it seems so brief
Clematis hanging from the trellis
Bareness of the walls relieve.
Colour everywhere resplendent
Green & Gold & Pink & Blue
Summer's really in it's fullness
Sending forth it's royal hue.

August now the Summer's closing
Cornfields their golden crop have shed
Gladioli stand erect like soldiers
In Pink & White & Mauve & Red.
Autumn's coming with September
Trees their leaves will turn to gold
But still the shades of Nature
Are a wonder to behold.
Onward now into October
Carpets of fallen leaves on the ground
Mainly Chrysanthemums and Roses
The only flowers to be found.
November bringing mist and frost
Any flowers now are lost
Their heads to black have turned
Onto compost heaps they are tossed
In December no flowers to be seen
But Wind & Frost & Snow
It's a time that we all have to wait
For next years flowers to grow.

AIR OF SPRING

Once again I sit alone
And greet the cold grey dawn
I'm feeling pretty drowsy
Lethargic and forlorn
The Winter's now upon us
Although it hasn't been too hard
There's only rain it's pouring down
Making puddles in the yard
But then again this time of year
It's weather you've expected
But when it goes on day 'on day
You're bound to feel dejected
I'm looking at the front garden
The weeds don't seem to grow
'tho the little English Marigolds
Their orange blossoms show
Although at night I've noticed
Their coloured heads they bow
I've often wondered why they do
Flowers seem to know somehow
In days from now some Daffodils
Crocus and Snowdrops too
The pretty variegated heads
will be showing through
Although the soil's still bitter cold
and other plants won't grow

These Mother Nature's children
Always seem to know
The trees they soon will start to bud
And leaves may well be seen
The branches are growing to support
Their wonderful cloak of green
All these thoughts are in my head
As I clear the mist of the night
That Spring is round the corner
I hope the picture I've painted is right.

12th January 2007

DEATH OF A CLOWN

For me my Life's been the theatre
A Thesbian I wanted to be
Treading the boards as a trouper
Join in the joviality
Each role I played was a pleasure
The applause gave a lift to my soul
The stage was my very existence
But now the years have taken their toll
No longer can I be "Top of the Bill"
But a "stand in" when they are short
Of players to play demanding roles
In the past for my position I've fought
Now I am faced with decision
Shall I wear the mask of drama to hide a frown
Or bring to conclusion this lonesome life
And end my life as a clown
As I slowly walk to the riverside
To slip in the water and drown
When all that is left to remember me
As my body sinks below
A few Daffodils float on the surface
As the finale to my Life's last show.

27th June 2008

ACUPUNCTURE

My shoulders are damaged in need of repair
I'll have to try something find someone to care
I make a phone call and speak to a friend
Acupuncture's worth trying it's the modern trend
I think for a while 'til my brain is quite numb
Are the needles my saviour, do I finally succumb
The appointment is made and I finally arrive
At the Pall Mall surgery, it's a very short drive
But while I was driving so deep was my thought
About the new treatment I'm about to court
I'm invited to enter by a young lady named Anne
As I sat in the chair the many questions began
Where is the damage what pain are you in
In her earnest endeavour just where to begin
As I sat on the couch my mind is aware
Of the Physio's fingers swiftly moving with care
Trying to find the source of my pain
To help me raise my arms easily again
My skin the needles are starting to pierce
Placed by hands with professional art
Are my shoulders just a pin cushion
Or is my recovery about to start
To the needles are added a small 'lectric charge
There's also some "ultra sonic"
I'm starting to wonder when it all ends
Will my shoulders become "bionic"
For 2 or 3 visits appointments are made
In the hope that the cure I've found
The pain in my shoulders has started to fade
Will my shoulders again be quite sound
After one more visit to the surgery
My treatment has come to an end
With "Physio" and Acupuncture
By a Professional Lady, a Friend.

19th June 2005

IN AN ENGLISH COUNTRY GARDEN

As I sat alone in a quiet room
I gazed from the window & stare
And saw Flowers in bloom
To form a floral picture there
Of a typical English Garden
The lawn now green from a Winter rest
Amongst Snowdrops and Tulips
Where Daffodils and Jonquils show best
Here and there some Marigolds too
Budding Roses standing bold
Creating a wonderful hue
Waiting their outer leaves to unfold
A sign of the loving Gardener's care
Keeping them free from bugs and mites
That seemed to fill the air
Which now is filled with a fragrant scent
Is this what Mother Nature meant
Or was it merely heaven sent
To an English Country Garden
The lawn is mowed to perfection
Not a weed nor clover is seen
Even the edges of the flower beds
Trimmed with a blade so keen
Shredded bark in abundance
Strewn on the Rose beds with care
In a concentrated effort to assure
No weeds are growing there

There's a sign of the Peonies nudging through
After their winter rest
Always hoping for a windless June
So they can look their best
Here and there among the flower beds
Fuchsias Blues & Mauves & Reds
Hoping their variegated heads
Will set up a radiant glow
But the Flower that is my favorite
From South Africa it came
Is the lovely Osteosternum
Or an African Daisy by another name
But I mustn't forget the stately trees
That afford the garden some shade
The Flowering Cherry, Apple and Pear
Their blossom and fruit well displayed
They are also haven to our feathered friends
Be it Summer Winter or Spring
And as you casually stroll in the Garden
Hear the lovely creatures sing
All a part of Nature's Rich Tapestry
Throughout the hours when it's light
But then comes the Shadow of Eventide
Followed by the silence of the night.

12th August 2008

HAND OF FRIENDSHIP

The open hand of friendship
Is something widely known
An open invitation
That's universally shown
To indicate to anyone
Of your inborn intent
Coupled with assurance
Of what is truly meant
You show offence to no-one
Without reason, without malice
For argument can soon flare up
And need peacemaker's chalice
Disputes are often futile
And solve nothing in the end
But the open hand of friendship
Will gain another Friend.

18th February 2007

Moving

I've only moved twice in my married life
After much planning and thought
We moved into a new Bungalow
That for £1700 we bought
And after nine years and two children
Our home was only quite small
Just a Bathroom, Kitchen Lounge and 2 Beds
And a narrow nine by three hall
So with bit in my mouth I made the decision
A new Chalet I was going to build
I didn't think there'd be problems
But all the doubts were soon killed
By the Park I picked a site with great care
But when it came to the planning
The Council deemed I should build a pair
The whole of the site they were spanning
The foundations I dug and the concrete I poured
14 hours a day was my task
Then brick after brick I layed with my trowel
Was my target, 2 months, too much to ask
When 4 weeks had passed the walls were all up
And on went the roof rafter by rafter
The Tiles and the floors, the doors and the Plaster
Then the heating and plumbing followed after
The "Sparks" and the Painter add the final touch
We met our goal and I'd like to explain
That as we were finished 39 years ago
I vowed never to move again.

28th June 2007

OFFSHORE

Dawn is breaking once again
Fishermen walking down the lane
Harbour wall is just in sight
As rising Sun replaces night
The tide is rising, buoys are bobbing
Fishing boat's old diesels are throbbing
Crew's aboard, they leave the shore
Out to search the shoals once more
There's work to do as they travel on
nets to mend and maintenance done
Wind is rising swelling the Tide
Bigger troughs and crests to ride
Radio begins to clatter
Fishing grounds are drawing near
Louder now the Skippers chatter
As other fishing boats show clear
Nets are running fast and free
Spewing into the foaming sea
Crew's alert for any snag
That might affect their catch.
Speed is down now, they start the trawl
The crew are stood at ease
Waiting to retrieve their nets
Hoping their catch will please
The order's given, the winches turn
Trawl's coming in now, over the stern
The tension is rising, the nets take the strain
As a voluminous catch lands in the holds again
Now its "Stow away the gear lads
Hose down the decks"
Everything's safe as the Skipper checks
Forward the throttle, hear the old diesels roar
All eyes to the coastline and Home once more.

17th October 1994

Part Two

War & Military

A selection of poems in the context of War, Military and Remembrance themes.

CHILDHOOD YEARS

As I sit on Sunday evening
With little on my mind
I tried to recollect
Some of the Memories left behind
To take that long walk back in time
When I was only three
And bought a bag of chocolate buttons
For just one half-penny
There were no thoughts of War then
And luxuries we never had
But Happiness was paramount
When I were but a lad
So on along Life's road I walk
To 1939
And War's declared in Europe
The bright lights no longer shine
'Tho young at heart I saw the difference
And noticed the growth of fear
As hostilities were extended
In little more than a year
Food was now on Ration
As an Island supplies were short
For a lot of the food we needed to live
We only acquired by Import
From other parts of the Commonwealth
South Africa and the U S A
Even Argentina had an important part to play
Of course the mode of travel then
Was across the Atlantic Ocean
But because of German U-boats & Navy
Armed convoys were set in motion
To guard their precious cargo
Too many Merchant ships were lost
Along with Naval vessels & crews

What an enormous price in lives lost
Undaunted they carried on their task
As did the RAF lads in the skies above
Relentless to repel the Luftwaffe
To save the Cities we all love
Civil Defence & Fire Service as well
Civilians too were joining the fight
Even the Air Raid Wardens

Saying "Oi, you! Put out that Light!"
But back to the children who now knew the strain
And witnessed Air Warfare
As the bombs continually rain
Down on their home Towns and Cities as well
Is this what it's like if you are living in Hell
Where once were rows of houses
Now huge craters in the ground
Death and destruction
Is all that can be found
But they carried on their young lives
As well as they could
For this sort of existence
Is all they understood
They went to school with Gas Masks
And in Air Raid Shelters they slept
Whilst Mum & Dad were sleepless
As their nightly vigil they kept
Then the youngsters were resilient
Not too worried at their plight
As they played in the Park in the daylight
And did their homework at night
There were smiles on their faces
And laughter and tears
As they carried on with their young lives
During those disastrous five years
So once again in Post War years
When hostilities cease

Did the children of Great Britain
Know the meaning of Peace
Now they can move forwards
On Life's road once more
In a peaceful environment
And free to explore
The pleasures that surround them
Never aware of the cost
That regaining their freedom meant
Many thousands of lives that were lost.

16th March 2008

FALL OF SINGAPORE

Now George was a man well known to me
A mild and gentle man
He was my brother in law you see
And when WW2 began
He like most young men enlisted
In the Army to fight the foe
Not ever knowing for sure
To which part of the world he would go
He joined the Essex Regiment
But wasn't there for long
He was transferred to the Suffolk's
And on a large troopship 'fore long
However before he bad his Wife goodbye
He was told he was going to be a Dad
And this was to stand him in good stead
When his future turned quite bad
For he was bound for Singapore
As reinforcements were in dire need
To fight the advancing Japanese Army
Travelling at alarming speed
Through the Burmese Jungles
Approaching Singapore from the rear
Defence was set for a seaborn attack
And created the Allies biggest fear
By the time George's convoy had landed
It was all too little too late
As they waited to repel the Japs at Changhi
On the golf Course they were left in a hell of a state
As they moved on the order to advance they were hit
By machine gun, shell and Mortar as well
And before they reached the halfway mark
Half of the regiment fell
Regroup cried the Officers and we'll try once again
And George had to run to HQ to request support

But he never made the journey
As in a mortar blast he was caught
And taken to Changhi Hospital
To patch up this wounded soldier bold
Till he regained conciousness
His mates had perished he was told
So now he was a POW of the dreaded Japanese
For they had over-run Singapore
They'd taken it with ease

They lived in concentration camps
Waiting for shipment to Japan
And this is where their life of terror
Truthfully began
George said they'd eaten anything
Chickens rats and snakes
As when you're really starving
A strong stomach is what it takes
And resolve to live as well you can
In order to survive
And return to "Blighty" when it's over
The reason to stay alive
They sailed to Japan eventually
Ship after ship with soldiers loaded
Antiquated vessels all rusty and corroded
They all worked hard in the daylight hours
Despite the lack of food
But they did there bit to upset their captors
When caught their punishment was crude
Boots and whips and rifle butts
Were the general methods they used
Any thought of Convention and Humanity
Were Oh ! so sadly abused
Eventually 4 years later the War was over
Via New Zealand and Australia by ship they came
Leaving behind so many of their colleagues

Fatalities to that nation of shame
When George left the shores of England
A fit young 12 stone man was he
And as he underwent a medical on his return
He weighed a mere 6 stone 3
To live a normal life again forever he would strive
As when he walked back into the arms of his wife
He saw his daughter for the first time and she was five
And even till the day he died
No malice did he bear
I've written this for you Benny Lim
As sadly George is no longer here.

6th September 2008

MINELAYER

In Memory of Chief Petty Officer Fred Maynard

In Felixstowe Docks many years ago
As the country was ready to sleep
There was a group of British seaman
With a dangerous rendezvouz to keep
At a time when World War 2
Was really at it's height
A small flotilla of minelayers
Had to cross the English Channel at night
To join them on their mission
M T B's and M G B's as well
Always ever hoping
There wouldn't be a heavy swell
As they made their arduos journey
Not knowing what they might meet
For they would be travelling with lights extinguished
In order to be discrete
With strict maintenance of silence
For this convoy of the night
The only contact with each other
A minimal stern blue light
The crossing it was Oh! so slow
To minimise the noise
A strain on all these Sailors
Some of them merely boys
The object of the exercise
A field of mines the layers to lay
In yet another attempt
To keep the enemy at bay
And finally they entered the target zone
To carry out their deadly task
And leave again intact
Is all the Skippers could ask

And just as they had finished
Someone fired a signal flare
Fired by a German E-boat
Who had come across them there
Immediately the order was given
Full throttle lads and home
At 25 or 30 knots this time
The Channel was awash with foam
Spewed out by those powerful engines
In ever roughening seas
The labouring Minesweepers
Led by the MTG boats & and awesome MTB's
Good fortune favoured the brave this night
As casualties there were few
And the air was full of sighs of relief
As the Harbour came into view
Events like these seldom come to light
As they were everyday events then
To highlight our need as an Island
For highly skilled Royal Naval men
To protect this sceptered Isle
From enemies far or near
Ever hopeful that another catastrophic war
Would not be a constant fear.

2nd July 2008

El Alamein

When I sit alone and close my eyes
Perhaps think of things long past
It is then I often visualise
How life has flown by so fast
My memory now is of a story
On which I will now recollect
A tale that was passed on many years ago
By a late friend, ex Soldier, I still respect
He told of a time he was shipped far away
On a troopship to Durban he sailed
Then up the East coast of Africa
In tropical kit regaled
But never knowing the Sahara desert
Their home was soon to be
Much less the many months and years
Before their Families they would see
They travelled far into this no-man's land
And formed a make believe Airstrip there
They encircled the perimeter with barbed wire
Ever conscious of attack from the air
They set up make believe tanks and aircraft
All covered with camouflage netting
But it all seemed real to the Lufwaffe
As seen by the air raids they were getting
Every day the Bulldozer driver
Formed an apparent runway in the sand
Giving an outsider the impression
That Allied planes would take off and land
The Royal Artillery lads did their bit on the Bofors
Keeping the Luftwaffe Fockerwolfs away.

As their raids became more persistant
Whether it be night or day
Then one day the Bulldozer driver

Still driving the machine to and fro'
Was subjected to an all out aerial attack
There was nowhere for him to go
The Bofors did their best to deter the attackers
Until the cowardly Fockerwolfs fled
All that was left was the shot up vehicle
And beside it the Gallant driver lay dead
He'd given his life for a make believe Airstrip
Was it really worth dying for
But perhaps it was the actions of men like these
That helped to shorten the desert campaign
To defeat Rommel and his Africa Corps
At the Battle of El Alamein.

9th October 2008

THE WHITE BERET

We're moored alongside the jetty
And the Captain's just come aboard
A quick last look at the dockside
Is all that we can afford
As the Skipper calls to the crew
"let go fore'ard" & "let go aft "as well
It's the start of another voyage
Which may take us to edge of hell
As escort Destroyer for a convoy
And for Russia we are bound
To make sure our group of merchantmen
Reach the destination safe and sound
Although we know that many of these ships
Ancient and in need of repair
Will never survive the journey
Because of the the dangers lurking there
Beneath the North Atlantic
The U-boats of Germany
Wreaking havoc on British convoys
From their sanctuary beneath the sea
To guard their precious vessels and cargoes
Is every Destroyers task
But to think of a trip without incident
Is a little too much to ask
Then suddenly an explosion and smoke, in plumes
Rise from the rearmost ship
The first torpedo's hit its mark
And the U-boat will try to slip
Away from the scene of carnage
'fore the Destroyer makes a full speed sweep
With salvo's of depth charges going down
To seek out this cowardly enemy of the deep
But they can also see the survivors of the blast
And no assistance can they give

For they know that should the Destroyer stop
Another crew of Sailors might not live
For there was ever the threat that the U-boat might return
Or another from the same pack.

Ever hopeful that they would get the chance
In another catastrophic attack
But once again they are on there way
In a very sombre mood, with the eyes of the operator
As though to the Sonar glued
Awaiting the sign of another submarine
Or even raiders from the air
As all Atlantic convoys suffered at length
Even with the greatest care and skill from unarmed sailors
In vessels that shouldn't really be there
But showed the resolve to fight and win
Rather than give in to despair
Their cargo's were desperately needed
As a lifeline in the theatre of war
With sometimes super human efforts
The like of which the World had not seen before
Time and time again as they journeyed through the sea
To that destination in Russia far away
They would witness once again, with terrible distain
The traumatic happenings of this day
But time and time again
Convoys travelled on this route and
Oh! so many ships and crews were lost
The outcome we now know was a victory
Paid for by Mariners at such enormous cost
To face these trips so many times
I feel it is fair to say
Those Sailors well and truly earned the right
To wear the coveted "White Beret".

In Memory of Chief Petty Officer Fred Maynard
26th June 2008

MEMORIES

When I was asked my Memory to jolt
And write of something past
My pen to paper quickly put
And words came think and fast
Though phrases and words
They simple might be
Through the eyes of a six year old child I see
peace is shattered
War's declared
To fight the enemy they're getting prepared
Its 1940 and here we see
The start of the Evacuee
In school playground children stand
Willingly taken by the hand
By Teachers, some with tears,
Because of young and tender years
To board the Buses, where are they going,
Children nor Parents even knowing
From the School down to the Station
ready for Evacuation
From the Buses we follow like sheep
The Teachers, who know we'll sleep
Away from Guns & Bombs & Slaughter
When country lanes will ring with laughter
On the train some children crying
From parents they've suddenly parted
With a shout from the Guard
And the Shriek of his whistle
Our mistery journey has started
The tears subside, the time is right
We children try to cuddle tight
From the windows we patiently watch
For a sign of where we are going, to catch
Another Cow, a Tractor, a Station

Perhaps we're nearer our destination
Out of the Train, onto the Coach
Down the lanes as we approach
The country village where we must stay.

To live, to learn and to play
In the Village Hall we stand and wait
For Villagers to decide our fate
hey look at the labels on our coats
Our name is all that it denotes
But it makes us look so humble
When asked our Names we can only mumble
Are we frightened, is it fear
We're so very tired, we don't really care
As they wander up and down the rows
For a glimpse of the child they'll eventually choose
Pretty Girls and charming Boys
Are finding homes quite fast
But the scruffy and the naughty ones
Are being left till last
The Hall is now quite empty
There's only five of us now
Three little brothers from Barking
And my Brother and I, somehow
When we left we gave Mother a promise
Together we'd stay, side by side
We wouldn't be separated
No matter how Villagers tried
The other boys have disappeared now
Our hopes are beginning to fade
When along came our substitute Parents
And a lifelong friendship was made
They kept us and fed us like sons of their own
A hardy and strenuous task
And all they got for the effort, 'cept our Love
Was "ten bob" a week, too much to ask?

1973

Dark Before Dawn

Autumn Came in '39
With an infamous day in September
Peace is shattered, War's declared
A day the whole World will remember
Chamberlain's failed to negotiate
Terms based on Britain's hopes
Time alone it seems will tell
How well the Nation copes
With Ration Books & Gas Masks issued
Air Raid Shelters supplied
Dug in the garden, installed in the House
So Civilian from Luftwaffe could hide
Dornier, Heinkel & Messchersmitt too
Nightly the Enemy arrived
Thousands of bombs fell like confetti
The 'planes engines screamed as they dived
Streets obliterated, Towns were destroyed
Their occupants killed or maimed
The Bulldog Spirit was resilient
Shaken, though not many complained
These attacks were finally thwarted
By our lads from the R.A.F.
And the reward most got for their efforts
Was an early and untimely Death
Searchlights Ac Ac Guns and Barrage Balloons
All played their part in this Fight
With Civil Defence and "Dads Army" Home Guard
An A.R.P. Warden shouts "Put out that Light"
The N.F.S. Firemen worked diligently
Each night as the City burns
Regularly joined by Salvation Army
With "buns" and "Tea" from their urns
Away from the Home Front the War carried on
On the Sea and the Desert as well

But Montgomery and the "8th Army"
Made sure, at Alamein, Germany fell

The Royal Navy played an important part
To guard each shipping lane
For, being an Island, we needed supplies,
Our War Effort to maintain
Wellingtons, Lancasters & Spitfires fly over
For hours each night it seems
To decimate Germany's Cities and Dams
And terminate the Fuhrers' dreams
With Britain's hopes higher, yet another threat
Slaughter rains from the Sky
Jet propelled Rockets and "Doodlebug" bombs
And once again thousands more die
But the tide of war changed with the advent of D.Day
Amidst gloom, a glimpse of the Sun
For the Allies gigantic Normandy invasion
Soon had the oppressors on the run
The War was soon over but not without cost
For many warriors never returned
PEACE came again to EUROPE
In "Blood, sweat and tears" it was earned.

21st February 1995

Armistice Day

It's 11 am on Armistice Day
A truly reverent scene
Row upon row of yesterday's Soldiers
Veterans now but just as keen
As they answered the call as young men & Women
To fight for the right to be free
From the possible threat of Dictators
Stealing their country's liberty
Year after year since 1918
ex Servicemen young and old
Return here to the Cenotaph
To remember fallen colleagues bold
They march so proud, with their heads held high
Chair bound and invalids too
To honour the dead and fallen
Brothers in arms through and through
Every possible Service represented there
Thinking as one, in accord
There were those who saved their homeland
Those who fought terrorism abroad
With their heads to the right, as they pass the Queen
To give the time-honoured salute
Today they're here to pay homage
From the Veterans to the raw recruit
They've come to a halt and there's silence
For the Service and then the wreath's are laid.

Then as one the heads and standards are lowered
Each in his own way prayed
In unison with the lone Bugler
As he blew the Last Post
Many with a tear on their faces
Remembering their personal Ghost
Of battles past when colleagues they'd lost
Tho' never far from their mind
And on an occasion such as this
Comfort and peace they can find
The call now comes for " Attenshun"
The Bearers their Standards now raise
The Old Soldiers march off in formation
To conclude one of Britain's proudest Military Displays.

9th November 2008

THE BRITISH SOLDIER

He left the shores of his homeland
In the service of the Queen
And as we headed out in the Channel
Behind us the White Cliffs of Dover seen
For the last time perhaps
In many a day, or even months or years
As he gazed at the wake behind him
In his eyes were just a few tears
A soldier he'd always wanted to be
Since a lad it had been his dream
To put on his boots and battledress
And be part of an Army team
Ready to fight for the right to be free
Of oppression and rid the terrorist threat
The task that lay before him
He'd not comprehended yet
Although he'd trained for many a month
At last he'd be put to the test
Fighting a foe on foreign soil
No quarter given to come out the best
But when we arrived at the foreign shores
We could hear the gunfire rattle
From Tanks and forward Artillery
Very soon we would join the battle
And now this lad just 18 years old
Witnessed war for the very first time
The heat, the hate, the torment
The smell, the noise and the grime
The terror as shells pass close over head
Their target too distant to see
But then a roar and a scream and a bang
Retaliation and our first casualty
It was his mate who had caught the fatal blast
Who he'd known not a month nor more

And they'd come here to practice what they had learnt
Then he died on a foreign shore
It was afterwards written by one of his mates
Don't bury him here in this land
But lay him to rest in the pleasant green pastures
Where his childhood dreams were all planned.

22nd February 2007

The Life Man

As my Service Life comes to a close
It brings forth a couple of tears
Where have they suddenly vanished
Those days in 22 years
I remember well the day I joined
The Service of my choice
The forbidding sight of the Guardroom
The volume of the Sergeant's voice
We were taken in hand by our Guardian
To instruct us on Service Life
Of the way to properly make our bed
Then lay out Kit, fork, spoon and knife
To don for the first time the Uniform
Be it Khaki or two shades of blue
To wear it with pride was the main thing
It didn't matter what the hue
To eat with the lads in the Mess Room
Or NAAFI for Tea and a "wad"
To hear someone shout "are you buying mine"
And answer "get your own you tight s!!d "
The Instructors were strict, but taught you a trade
Your welfare always on their mind
Even took care of slow learners. extra classes
Making sure they were not left behind
The Tests are all finished and Tradesman are we
Ready to fight the good fight
Always hoping, to kill we'd not have to
But knowing sometime that we might
Be called to Active Engagement
To fight for a worthy cause
And know that if the battle you won
There'd be no room for applause
For in War it is inevitable, we all know
The ultimate price that some pay

To lay down their life for their Country
To improve life for others some way
But then there were times we remember
Like when we were out on the Town
Having a few "bevvies " at the "Local"
And trying our worries to drown.

Ever alert for "Redcaps" or "Snowdrops"
Always on the look out for trouble
Knowing that if they catch you, adrift
It's up to the C.O "at the double"
"fizzers" & "jankers" were par for the course
Once you'd heard the C.O's sentence
Then you vowed that "never again", would kick in
And at least a week of repentance
Tho' then there were the serious times
Of battles won and lost
In the heat of battle you hadn't time
To stop and count the cost
But now as you stare at the Medals you've won
And know that you'll wear them with pride
To be able to stand in Silent Tribute
In Honour of the Lads & Lasses that died
For the time has now come, to walk slowly away
As the Barrack gates close behind
With the knowledge that a Life of Service, to the Queen
Is Eternally locked in Your Mind.

14th April 2007

CHANGING FACE OF WAR

Gone are the days when the warrior bold
Sat astride his trusty steed
Armed with a sabre of steel so cold
To thwart the enemy, his deed
And as we study how an Army life
Has changed over Oh! so many years
With crossbows, shot and musket
And even lances and spears
Progressing to formation of Infantry
With Rifles and bayonets at the ready
With riveting order of the Sergeant
"Come on lads hold the line steady"
Motorised armed units then came to the fore
As support to the lads on the ground
In the ever changing strategies of War
With experts ready to expound
Their theories on the rights and wrongs
On how best to carry out the task
When "Give us the tools and we'll do the job"
Was what the WW2 Squaddies used to ask
Battles would start with a barrage of fire
From hosts of Artillery
To weaken the positions and strongholds
Of a resourceful enemy
Followed by wave upon wave of support
From their colleagues in the air
And when the target is secured and overrun
The Tommy with rifle, and tin helmet was there.

But today there are weapons of mass destruction
Chemicals and missiles too you will find
In the changing method of warfare
So lethal and deadly defined
But still you will see the foot soldier
Fighting for peace and may die
Saying don't bury me here in these foreign fields
But in England's green pastures let my body finally lie
Don't weep for me at my graveside
For we are ne'er far apart
And though I've departed this world, that we know
I'll live for evermore deep in your heart.

25th June 2008

THE NATIONAL SERVICEMAN

World War 2 was long over
The Oppressors threat was past
But still mandatory for National Servicemen
To join a Military Force so vast
Occupations they're forced to leave
Where they'd worked since they were boys
Conscripted to Military Service
And they were given no choice
Except for which colour Uniform
Would they like to choose
Would it be the Army Khaki
Or one of the shades of Blues
Many left home for the first time
Not knowing what to expect
A totally new experience
To be taught the meaning of respect
Issued Uniforms, Allocated beds
Then down to the Barbers Shop
To get their shaven heads
When they stood on the square
Everything would be fine
As long as no hair showed
Below the new Beret line
They practiced and drilled
For hour after hour
To hear the Drill Sergeant shout
"You bloody horrible shower"
A term of endearment you later found out
Used at will on raw recruits
As NCO's pleasure was to yell & shout
Polish your brass and get a shine on those boots
Conscripts and Regulars together trained
As Soldiers, Airmen and Sailors to be
They would serve the Flag, their Country and Queen

These men of the Military
The lads of the day all mixed in together
Tho a barrier I think it is fair to say
And that was blatantly obvious
In the different levels of pay
The wage of a National Serviceman
Was a mere £1.8 shillings per week
Less 4 shillings for Barrack Room damages
Which I used to think was a cheek.

However at that time a Regular Serviceman
A princely £2.12 shillings would receive
And they also had another advantage
As they were allowed more Annual Leave
The N S man served for only two years
The Regular 3, 5 12 years or life
But they were truly brothers in arms
When it came to times of strife
The theatres of war I remember
As tho' it were only yesterday
Korea, Malaya and Borneo
Where comradeship came into play
The trade that they learned as a raw recruits
To obey those words of command
In order to survive the conflicts
And not perish in some Foreign Land
For their Enemies were not selective
Their sole objective was to kill
It mattered not what kind of Service Man
These marksmen would use their skill
In an effort to conquer our Peace Keeping Forces
The Terrorists no quarter would give
But the Battle seasoned Sergeant would never give up
To make sure all his troops would live
Regulars and National Servicemen side by side
But sadly some of the missions were lost

And many of Britain's young men died
Their sacrifice for Peace a terrible cost
So looking through those Conscriptive years
Were I an opinion to give
I believe it was a transition from boy to man
To return as a Civilian to live
For some a harsh lesson in reality
In Uniform there's so much to learn
Especially for the Conscript looking for Demob
And to his chosen career return.

6th November 2008

ROYAL BRITISH LEGION

It's Armistice Day in November
And Memories don't seem to fade
Time once more for Remembrance
And the Royal British Legion Parade
With their heads held high and shoulders back
There's a hint of sadness in their eyes
Still smart are these "Yesterday Soldiers"
Tho' they now wear suits and ties
Gone for them are the days of Uniform
The Khaki, The Navy and The Blue
Each served the Queen and the Country
All Britain's good men and true
And as they are called to attention
The Bearers their Standards raise
And march to the Local Memorial
In a silent moment each man prays
Then as one the Group of Bearers
Slowly let their Standards fall
As tho' in a quiet answer
To the lonely Buglers Call
And the familiar words they all remember
"At the going down of the Sun"
The universal words for those that were lost
We remember them, every one
So now it's back to attention
With medals on their chests well displayed
As they march away in grand formation
In the Royal British Legion Parade.

18th July 2007

63RD ANNIVERSARY OF D DAY.

All the ships are in the harbours
With our armaments they are filled
Ever at the ready to sail
With a readiness that's instilled
In every British fighting man
With his duty to rout the foe
And now the waiting is over
And it's time for the Aramada to go
Hundred upon hundred
Of Britain's young fighting men
Across the Channel what will they find
Will they ever come home again
And this was uppermost in their mind
As the Normandy coast they neared
The opposition far worse than anyone feared
Many were lost 'fore they landed
And many died on the beach
In the terrible salvo's of shells and mortar
Thro' the air as they constantly screech
But undeterred our lads carried on
Through the gunfire, the smoke and the stench
And occasionally stop to take cover
To have a "fag" or sip of water in a trench
For their bodies were aching and their lips were parched
With a limited amount of transport
Each day they carried on and marched
With every day the advance that they made
Was greeted with the "locals" admiration
For the lads of the British Army
Who had come to rescue their war torn Nation
Eventually the Germans were ousted.

But at a truly dreadful cost
Which was paid by the British Liberation Army
And the thousands of lives that were lost
In order to end the war of all wars
Or so they were led to believe
But now we all know in reality
Impossible to achieve
And so if you all just close your eyes
And imagine if you can
The 6th of June 63 years ago
And the fate of the British Military Man
As you know there are those few survivors
Who trek to Normandy year on year
With their heads that are bowed and tears in their eyes
Thinking "Fred, Dick or Harry are you still here"
The debt that we owe is enormous
A price we cannot afford to pay
But we can now bow our heads in silence
And remember the lads not here with us today.

5th June 2007

RETROSPECT

In War there is one winner
The Grim Reaper is his name
In retrospect it's easy
On who to lay the blame
But in these British Islands
Soldiers true we've trained
To carry out their daunting task
So peace may be maintained
'tho we all know impossible
Is what their goal may seem
They carry out their chosen role
And win worldwide esteem
As any troubled Nation through time
Our assistance they may ask
To rid them of a coup d'etat
Or Terrorism may be their task
But politicians never fight
It's only they who decide
Like Chamberlain, Churchill & Thatcher
Who will fight for this Country's pride
And if we asked of the men of that time
Would they all agree it was right
For them to lay their lives on the line
I've a feeling that they just might
In retrospect say what is war all about
What is the goal that we seek
To rid far off Nations of oppressors
And give protection to the weak.

Part Three

Odes

*A selection of Poems recording the complex lifestyles of
ex-Service Ladies, Wives and Daughters*

A LASSIE'S DREAM

Is there ever a time when you sit and think
Of how your life could have been
Would you really have altered many things
For many you couldn't have foreseen
Think to the times when a Lass at school
Many a laugh you had with your mates
Or perhaps there was a special someone
You'd meet at the garden gates
Of the times you'd go to parties
Perhaps even your first dance
And the lads with their standard chat-up lines
Hoping you'd give them a chance
Of a date to go to the Cinema
Or just an innocent walk in the Park
But always with a warning from your Dad
To make sure you were home by dark
But your mind travels on to the lad that you met
Who from your feelings you tried to hide
And then the inevitable happened
And Prince Charming asked you to be his Bride
From there the two of you travelled on
Your inspiration a Service life
For your Husband a career in the RAF
And for you a Serviceman's Wife
At first the time it seemed to stand still
Each moment you were living your dream
But then the years gathered momentum
And the speed that they passed was extreme
In that time you had many a laugh
And I dare say you shed a few tears
Not least as you looked back at the Guardroom, for the last time
Where have they gone those 38 years
So now you have to move forward
To a full life in "civvy street"

Knowing it could be a daunting task
New colleagues and friends to meet
But instead of staying in Barracks or Quarters
A house of your own you'd acquire
Away from the humdrum of the City
With a nice garden where you'd sit and retire

Tho' now and again life has it's snags
And the hand that you're dealt may seem rough
Adversity often builds extra determination
To fight when the going gets tough
I thought these words I'd write for you Dear Friend
Because I honestly & truly believe
When you've read them it will give you a lift to your Life
Especially as it's CHRISTMAS EVE.

24th December 2007

BRANDY.

Her story started long ago
Is something I must explain
Grandad, a Musician came from Turkey
And Grandmother came from Spain
Now Dad he was a Midlands man
From Retford in Nottingham he came
Enlisted in the Army
And took a number for his name
He joined the Royal Corps of Signals
Without too many fears
Finished his time as Warrant Officer 1
After serving 31 years
But during his time he met Joya, from Jerusalem
The young lady was to become his Bride
To live the life of an Army Wife
And always be there by his side
Then in 1944 in Wartime London
By way of a surprise
There baby daughter Barbara was born
The apple of their eyes
They set their mind on a Family
For more children they were keen
Then brothers Donald and Kenneth came into this world
And also a lovely sister named Jean
They grew up like most Families do
Through their childhood years
Times when the air was filled with laughter
But sometimes sadness and tears
Now schooling was a varied affair
In Lincoln, Nottingham and Dorset
Then there was Yorkshire and Devonshire too
Their education to reinforce it
With Mum & Dad they travelled the World
West Africa, Malaya and Cyprus

Even Germany as well
And that's where Barbara met her Husband
Or so I have heard folks tell
Her Dad was the lads RSM
And he thought of this Son-in-Law fine
Woe betide this Soldier bold.

If he ever steps out of line
In June 1966 the Happy Couple were wed
And settled to Military life
'cos now it was young Barbara's turn
To become an Army Wife
Together they had two lovely children
Daughter Tina and Robert their Son
They knew that after these two additions
That their Family life had begun
Dressmaking, Sudoku and reading
Hobbies that Barbara enjoyed
She also liked Middle of the Road and Country Music
Can't remember if she mentioned Pink Floyd
Then Tina & Robert grew and married
As most young couples do
And then over the ensuing years
Babs had 4 Grandchildren too
The bit that I missed in the middle
Was that Babs joined the T A for 2 years as well
There's a Military trend in the Family
That isn't too hard to tell
So now as I come to a conclusion
And bring this tale to an end
I like to wish health and happiness to you and your Family
From Shrubby your Internet friend.

September 2008

CASSIE

Once upon a time in Stockton on Tees
Oh!Many many years ago I know
A young couple yearned for a child of their own
When would this wee bairn show
Then all of a sudden out of the blue
One bright and sunny morn
Can you guess what happened,
Yes!! Our Carol "Cass" was born
She was the pride of her Parents eye
Who cuddled her and kept her warm
Kept her clothed and fed as well
Making sure she came to no harm
I think that she had Sisters, four
And was also blessed with a Brother
This was surely a Happy Family
A credit to Father and Mother
But then as babies always do
Young Carol quickly grew
At School she learnt, played with Dolls as well as other Toys
Then as her teenage years approached
Took an interest in the Boys
This time in life goes quickly by
And a career comes into her mind
So she chose a stint in the WRAF
And left the lads behind
Two years she spent in Uniform
And served the Country, Flag & Queen
And probably travelled around
To places she'd never been
But all things come to an end, they say
And as Carol passed the Station Gates
She turned and wiped away a few tears
As she waved goodbye to her mates
So onward she stepped into "Civvy Street"

Her feet were really itching
She would try and find a suitable job
Which was solved by working in a Kitchen
She married too, to a loving Hubby
In the house there was always plenty of noise
For this was another thing that I learnt
Carol had three loving boys
Three sons who later got married
And set up homes of their own
Where love was there in abundance
As 6 Grand-children have shown
A widow now but she still carries on
With Life, as we all have to do
And the Lads are there for encouragement
Making sure she pulls thro'
When she comes home from work in the evening
She'd sit in front of the Telly and knit
Perhaps listen to the Beatles and 60's music
While asked to Baby-sit
To cover the life of someone on paper
A person you've not even met
I hope that I've painted your picture, with words
Just a friend on the Internet.

20th April 2008

ODE TO THE CELTIC MAIDEN

In Wales as the words of the song says
A welcome in the hillside we'll keep
For the people who visit our country
To see the Mountains & Valleys and sheep
Which are always on mind as you travel
Through the Welsh countryside
They say counting them helps you to sleep
But Tom came from the Emerald Isle
Met Madge and settled in Hirwaun
A pleasant little village near Aberdare
Where there Daughter Theresa was born
As the couples first born
She's their joy and their pride
That nobody can dispute
'cos Tom always reckoned his little daughter
With Red Hair, was as pretty as she was cute
But time moves on and to school she was sent
At St. Margaret's Primary R C
And as Magdalene was a teacher
Theresa's schooling was priority
She did all the things that little girls do
Including music and dancing and sport
So much to cram into those early years
For childhood is really quite short
Then as a teenager, when Schooling had finished
It was time to make up her mind
To choose a career as an adult
What were the choices she'd find
Should she work in a Shop, or Receptionist be
Or work in a factory on a machine
But Theresa dismissed all these options
To serve in the WRAC for the Flag and the Queen
Six years in the Uniform of Khaki
Really suited her fine

And spent some of her service in Germany
With the British Army of the Rhine.

Now during this time Bill came into her life
He stole her heart and they were wed
And in 1987 Theresa left the WRAC
To become a civilian instead
She carried out a housewife's duties well
Which including making a "cuppa"
After spending her daytime hours
As Area Manager selling Tupper
Reading, Music, entertaining and dancing
With the occasional Indian, Italian or Chinese
Which made a nice change from potato crisps
Or a nice slice of bread an cheese
But all this was soon to change it seems
As her darling son James was born
But Theresa never told me
Whether they'd returned to Hirwaun
Life as a Mum took up all her time
Until that time in 2003
When she made an Executive decision, to study
To become a Therapist, Complimentary
And went on to form a commercial enterprise
In order to practice her Therapy
Then opened a second venture
Both now running successfully
Now I haven't mentioned Mrs Campbell or Max
Tamla Motown, Jarreg or Bob Dylan and such
'cos to include all of these items
Might really seem too much
For anyone to read these lines already over laden
It gives me poetic licence to finish
My Ode to the Celtic Maiden.

11th June 2008

CRICKET LOVELY CRICKET

I sit at the computer
And gaze at the screen
And log into a Chatroom
Where often I've been
And type out a message
To friends that are unseen
There's some serious banter
And a laugh in between
Then on one occasion
Bella came in one night
So I casually asked her
If a poem should I write
And include some of the things
That I know she enjoys
Apart from housekeeping
And a chat with the boys
About her life in the Forces
How her life's changed since then
And I assume it's the same
For the Women as the Men
Except when you're a civilian
It's a change hard to make
But life still has its problems
As the long road you take
Now Bella it seems
'tho female may be
She likes to watch Cricket
Sometimes on T V
But if the weather is nice
In the hot Summer Sun
You'll find this young lady
In a deck chair having fun
Watching the lads
As they run 'twixt the wicket

Scoring lots of runs
In a bold game of Cricket
Then into the Beer Tent
With a shout of "Encore"
You will find our lady Bella
Having just one glass more.
And here I must end
These few words of rhyme
And hope you'll enjoy them
Time after Time.

Gail the Girl from Omagh

How can you start to write an Ode
About some young lady you don't even know
Well that's the task I've set myself
Just a day or two ago
It all began in the Emerald Isle
A good many years ago
When Mum & Dad in wedded bliss
Waited for their Family to grow
Then into this world came this lovely wee girl
The pride & joy of her Mum
Who'd spent all those many months
Waiting for baby to come
But infancy lasts but a very short while
And soon a grown girl was she
For she played with her toys
Had a laugh with the boys
And soon a teenager she would be
Procedure is something we all follow
But in this case I must say I would fail
'cos it was rather remiss of me, I forgot
To tell everybody her name was Gail
Who by now after long consideration
Had decided a move she should make
Away from the home stead in Omagh
Unsure which route she should take
But finally her mind was made up
And a Service life she would try
So she joined Queen Alexandra's Nursing Corps
And Oh! how the years seemed to fly
She served with the Military here and there
And in Nursing she did aspire
Then after 6 years Service
Gail decided it was time to retire
And return to normal life as civilian

With a salary so she could afford
All the little luxuries she was used to
While she was living abroad
But she didn't return to the Erin Isle
This lovely fair colleen
But decided to work and live in Germany
On working abroad she was keen
And in the evenings she likes to listen
To the music of Celine Dion
And does puzzles, reads books, takes care of her looks
In case she meets Sir Cliff Richard e'er long
So now as I write the penultimate lines
I must say how much pleasure I get
Out of writing these little Customised Odes
For my friends on the Internet.

15th April 2008

Helen another Wee Scottish Lassie

Can you picture the scene
All those years ago
Tho' how long I'm not quite sure
When a Bonnie wee Lass
And a Braw Scottish Laddie
Were Wedded for evermore
And then came along
A Bonnie wee bairn
And Helen was her name
The subject of this wee poem
And how into this world she came
Her Daddie was a hard working man
Each day to the Mine went he
To labour and toil to bring up the coal
For the country's prosperity
Her Mam would do what all Mothers do
To bring their children up right
To wash and feed and take them to School
And tuck them in bed each night
And onwards went Helen
From Childhood to teens
Till Womanhood came in sight
What Career would fill that void
A Service Life just might
And it wasn't long before she donned
Her Uniform for the first time
Became part of the WRAF
To travel the world beyond
The well known Scottish borders
Which had long been her abode
And now she'd cast care to the wind
To travel Life's rocky road
At night in the NAAFI she's quite content
To listen to the Music and chat

About Elvis her favourite Pop Star
Oh! Really how about that
Ever aware of the thrill of the Air
An avid flyer was she
And even jumped from the plane, by 'chute
Like a bird in the air she was free.
But as is the way of most things in life
All good things come to and end
And this happened to our Helen
When no longer would she defend
The Queen, The Flag and the Country
She'd served for so many years
And as she passed through the gate
For the very last time
No doubt she shed a few tears
So she's settled now in Civilian Life
Always willing to take advice
She's studying like a Woman possessed
And enjoying skating on ice
The fullness of life is hers, I believe
As I bring this Ode to and end
It's been a pleasure to write these few words in Rhyme
To Helen... an Internet Friend.

10th April 2008

I WERE JUST A SCOTTISH ARMY GIRL

This tale is of a Scottish lassie
A bold wee bairn was she
The pride of a loving Daddy
As she bounced on her Mammie's knee
She did the things wee Lassies do
And even went to school
By then it was very noticeable
She'd be nobody's fool
To be out in the Garden
Was always a delight
Rather than being stuck indoors
With her homework every night
But soon the teenage years were past
Time to make up her mind
Which Career might lie ahead
What occupation would she find
And in her head a vision
Although 'til now unseen
This bonnie wee Scottish lassie, in Uniform
For the Flag, the Nation and the Queen
Her way of life changed drastically
As into the Army she enrolled
To join the country's fighting strength
What wonders would life unfold
I think that Maria is her name
But she's called by the name of Maz
And I wondered if that's acquired as a nickname
That every Squaddie has
Now Service life is always a shock
And no less to a wee girl
Who's left her home for the first time
Her head in is a whirl
So on we move and training's past
What trade or occupation will she take

'cos she's very good with vehicles
A good M T Driver she would make
But she is always one for a laugh
And getting up to pranks.

She's twisted the Sergeants arm
And now she's even driving Tanks
Tho' on to trailers she loads them
And to Maz it's a bit of fun
But it's a good job she doesn't drive them into Battle
And fire the "B!!!!!!dy! big gun
She always kept herself in shape
For Athetics she was heaven sent
So many times she was nominated
To represent the Regiment
And not her only achievement
With other hobbies she would trifle
If you set up the target on the firing range
Was very good with a rifle
But all good things must come to an end
After 12 years, demobbed was she
And once again she had to think
Now what in civilian life can I be
She can't just sit in the garden
With a sandwich and a glass of wine
Knowing that is inevitable
For the Service life she would start to pine
She pondered the opportunities
Thought "What lies ahead for me"
Then she donned a Policeperson's uniform
And worked on Security
She never told of her Army life
Or whether she bore any scars
But the one thing I know for certain
Is she likes to be driving fast cars
There are probably many things I could write

But I'd only be having a guess
As Maz is a friend on the internet
And I a poor Internet Poet no less
Now there's one thing I definitely know
And I can say this without a shadow of doubt
That Maz adores "Neeps, Tatties and Haggis"
And with that said I think I'll sign out.

24th March 2008

JOANNE THE FAIR COLEEN FROM THE EMERALD ISLE

There's a lovely Irish couple
And I know they're gonna smile
If they ever read this ode
About the dear old Erin Isle
As they cast their minds back
To when their little girl was born
They never said exactly when
Afternoon or morn
For Dad it was a worrying time
Pacing to and fro'
But it gave him time to think
And he called his baby Daughter Jo
That was the shortened version
Of the lovely name Joanne
Abbreviated frequently
So that is how Jo began
She went thro' school and did the things
That children often do
Like pushing prams and playing dolls
With a nice bag of sweets to chew
But all these things are long since past
To a lady she has grown
Travelling rapidly thro' life
And may have a family of her own
I know that Cards mean a lot to her
Though the details I know not
But she's also interested in stitching
And sewing and Tapestry and the lot
Of things that a Seamstress may do

She's also a lover of animals
Dogs maybe one or two
But also heard from my secret source
She likes a Brandy to settle her down
She's a fair coleen from the Emerald Isle
Dances jigs in her Emerald Green Gown.

4th April 2008

Karen ex–Essex Girl

The scene is set this very night
A verse is on my mind
Travelled out to Colchester
To see what I could find
And there they were a nice young couple
Fowler I believe was their name
Shirley was an Essex Girl
But John, a Scot, from Edinburgh came
To play for Colchester United
Professional Football was his game
Mrs. Fowler was a tracer in an Office
 Paxman's was the company name
And then like most young couples do
With starting a Family on their mind
Their lovely young daughter Karen was born
Then brother Scott followed on behind
They grew up like most children do
Under their parents watchful eyes
Boys with toys and girls with Dolls
Burt it is hard to generalise
Then onward went Karen to a Convent School
Which she didn't find much fun
As she never really accepted her education
Being under supervision of a Nun
Other schools followed
Life was just a blur
For this young lady had decided that
Schooling was not for her
Tried her hand at Hairdressing
Found that rather glum
So she changed to being a Barmaid, in a Pub
For a higher weekly sum
Fate dealt a cruel blow when she was just 16
At 42 years old her Dear Dad John died

As he was the light and love of her life
And her feelings she tried to hide
But heavy drinking was not the answer
To the problem she had to solve
Then she thought about a Prince Charming
Which suitor would this involve
Most girls have thoughts of their Mr Right
That is normally so plain to see
But in Karen's case it was different
She actually married three.

No.1 was a REME man
With him there were children twice
A lovely daughter Michelle
And her charming brother Stuart was nice
In their eight years of Marriage
A true Military man was he
For when he left the Army
He joined the RAFP
Not much to say of Hubby No 2
The union was so very short
And Hubby No 3 lasted 4 years
For Karen this was a lesson taught
She carried on life as a single girl
28 years as the Controller Supreme
Sorting the problems of Taxi Drivers
To keep the Company's esteem
Now Karen has moved to Lewis in Scotland
Nearer her children to be
And make up for the lost times that they missed
She'll have to wait and see
Michelle is happy with a Restaurant to run
The RAF Regiment Stuart joins in the New Year
Perhaps this is the start of Karen's settled life
There'll still be the occasional tear
Mum Shirley's still about but they seldom meet

But as long as she's healthy that's just fine
Karen's got Music and Football and Formula 1
With Oasis, Take That, Boyzone to sing the last line
Now Lucy she is Her Brother's wife
With Niece Erin and Nephew Ben
The Stroke that Karen suffered 2 years ago
Fate had struck a cruel blow once again
She's left partially sighted and some fingers are numb
But it's blatantly obvious to see
That this November Girl is resilient
As all good Scorpios should be
And now as this tales comes to an end
I hope tragedy Karen will discard
As I wish her a long, Happy and Healthy life.
From Shrubby The Essex Bard.

30th October 2008

LANG MAE YER LUM REEK NOW.

There's a young Scots lassie I know
We met merely by chance
She had entered a Website Chat room
Maybe her life to enhance
A place where you meet folks
From near far and wide
They can open their hearts
'cos there's nothing to hide
A spare minute here
Or an hour or two
An acceptable pastime
When you've nothing to do
But sit at the screen
And type at your leisure
Some topics are serious
But most are for pleasure
And this particular young lady
Loves music and song
She types away at random
'tho she's singing along
And over her shoulder
When she turns on the Cam
You might see her Buddahbabe
Eating Egg Chips and Ham
Poetic licence allows menu to alter
When you run out of subject
And the poem might falter
So you write on regardless
As you know you just might
See Adele in the Chat room
When Alex is working at night
Lang mae yer lum reek now
As this story I'll end
It's your personal Poem
From your Internet Friend.

EVERY LITTLE BREEZE SEEMS TO WHISPER LOUISE

I don't know much about her
And I really shouldn't doubt her
As a nice young lass she's always seemed to me
So now if I'm allowed
I know that she'll be proud
Of the Ode I'm going to write about Louise
On a day many years ago
Exactly when I just don't know
Another lovely wee girl was born
She was the pride of Daddy's eye
And I know the reason why
He could cuddle her in his arms each morn'
As he tried to do his best
To give poor Mum a rest
And perhaps avoid dear Wifey's scorn
In his Arms he held her tight
As he put her in her cot each night
He would give her that last little squeeze
Then it came to Mum one night
As Dad had hoped it might
I know we'll call our baby girl Louise
So on we go thro' childhood
With Dolls & Bike & Toys
Then all of this she forsakes
And takes up dating with the boys
Now there's a thing when you live in Portsmouth
And it's a likely probability
When you're looking for employment
You'll finish up going to Sea
So Louise she joined the Navy
As a Wren in the Service of the Queen
And turned out in her Uniform
Smart as you've ever seen
But one night she was found aboard a ship

Tho' the reason I can't enlarge
She finished up before the Captain, on orders
Found guilty and duly charged
From Pompey to Culdrose and Plymouth
The time just seemed to fly
But at one of these establishments
A Marine Commando did espy
And after a couple of outings
Found him to be a really nice guy
And he became her "other half"
I'm not sure but I do believe
When I spoke to her on the Net one night
She said his name was Steve
But while I've been writing this story
I've noticed the lack of noise
'cos another thing Louise told me one night
She's the Mother of two growing boys.

6th April 2008

MISS ANN JONES

Wales is the land of Music & Song
Or so some people say
It was certainly the home of this happy couple
After their Wedding Day
Wesley was a Welshman true and proud
Whilst Margaret from England came
To build a marital home in Wales
And get used to her new Welsh name
They lived their new life as couples do
Perhaps with some children in mind
First a boy and then a girl
And another boy and girl followed behind
There was Anthony and Ann and Ian
All at the front of the queue
I nearly forgot to mention their Baby
A lovely young girl named Sue
Mum & Dad were proud of their Family
My 2 Brothers, my Sister and me
We did all the things that children do
Except for my Brother Anthony
He spent a lot of his time in Hospital
Whilst we could go out and play
The games that all the children do
And go to school each day
But childhood raced by so quickly
Then teenagers we all became
Sports and dancing and Music
That was the name of the game
I used to enjoy a good book to read
Or perhaps a long country Hike
But as I reflect on this Hobby
It might have been quicker by bike
I felt that the time had now come
For me to leave my Family home

To seek a new Career for myself
And perhaps the World to roam
But sadly at about this time
Mum & Dad decide to part
At such a crucial time in my life
It almost broke my heart
I thought a Military girl I'd be
All the details I had seen
This was the time I joined the WRAF
To serve The Country, The Flag and The Queen.

T'was during my time in the Service
That I found a Fiancé, it must be said
And after a normal courtship
In 1974 we were wed
After 3 years of marriage
The end of Service life for me
The plan was really quite simple
To start a Family
But the idea was fraught with danger
Which at the time I could not see
My ever loving Husband was having an affair
With someone other than me
So that was the end of my married life
From thereon I was on my own
To live the life of a single girl
And used to my own company I've grown
I'm still in touch with my Brothers and Sister
But Mum I seldom see
Tho' I know that she is happy and healthy
Which is a comfort to me
Four years ago Anthony passed away
At least he's now free from a life of pain
Sometimes I'm alone and I close my eyes

And he's here with me once again
I thought that I'd taken a few knocks in my life
On my health it was starting to tell
When yet once more Fate had taken a hand
My Dear Dad Wesley passed away as well
He fought long and hard to stay with me
As my Dad as well as a Friend
So I did everything that I could
To comfort him to the bitter end
But life must go on, or so they say
Tho' memories never die but fade
For life is built on love
And it's many ways displayed
Perhaps one day my Prince will come
And whisk me off into the night
Stories should have a happy ending
So for me it just might
The end of this Ode must be very near
So if I now sit and think really hard
While the curtains slowly draw to a close
Pulled by Shrubby the Essex Bard.

17th October 2008

"OLD BIDDY"

Now Dad he was an Army man
Right from the very start
And stationed down in Canterbury
He stole my Mothers heart
But this was Oh! so long ago
In those far off '30's days
And Mum & Dad would walk out together
And into each others eyes would gaze
It wasn't long before they were Wed
Their Union seemed like Heaven
Especially when little Sheila arrived
Some time in 1937
Dad left the Army for some time
The along came World War 2
And he answered the call to Colours
As any Military man would do
But his little daughter was only 3 years old
When she waved her Daddy goodbye
And she became her Mothers saving grace
Saw many a tear in her eye
But childhood in War is not easy
Normality you lose
You learn to live in deprivation
There's no other way to choose
For everyone around you life is the same
Get by the best way you can
To get over the various shortages
Food Rationing began
But Mum made sure that Sheila was fed
And supplied with presents and Toys
Enjoyed her days in the Classroom
With all the other girls and boys
Her Daddy was posted to the Middle East
From which he never returned

For he lost his life in battle in Leros
In 1943 was what Sheila learned
So now she had to be strong with her Mum
For she was all that mother had
They would always have the Memories, tho
Of her darling Soldier Dad.

Together side by side into teenage years
Each on the other depends
Not so much Mother and Daughter
More like very good friends
Then Sheila decided the WRAF she would join
For 3 years a Military Typist was she
At Wilmslow, Credenhill, Compton Bassett and Hawkinge
Were the postings that she would see
And after leaving the Service
Sheila met & married a man from the RAOC
It seems the Army is in the blood
Perhaps it's hereditary
After a while 2 Sons came along
With plenty of laughter and noise
This is the sort of thing to expect
As the Mother of two strapping boys
There were cats Minnie and Solo, Gerbils Herbert and
Sherbert
And even two dogs Pepe and Suzy
It seems that when lots of pets you acquire
With names you have to be choosey
There was Chicago, Bread, Elton John and Elvis
The music of Earl Bostic, Jim Reeves, Neil Diamond as well
Agatha Christie books, Rod Stewart singing "Sailing"
Sheila's versatile you can tell
She's travelled to many parts of the World
Sightseeing is one of her joys

But the ultimate gift to Sheila
I'm sure is the love of her two grown up boys
As she lives every day to the full now
And on the note I'd like to end
This tale of "Old Biddy" Sheila Luesley
And sign it from " An Internet Friend".

23rd September 2008

POLLYWOLLY DOODLE ALL THE DAY

We're looking back in time now
Quite a time before the War
Somewhere in Derbyshire
There's a couple I'm looking for
Courted in the early 30's
Or so I've heard it said
And after months or years maybe
The Happy Couple were wed
Then doing what most couples did
And the Wife would wash, cook and clean
Until they started a Family
With a young baby girl named Pauline
Times in the late 30's were very hard
And when she was only 3 years old
Her Daddy left to join the RAF
Or that is what I'm told
As World War 2 had started then
Her childhood world had altered
So Mum had to take the leading role
In which she never faltered
She went to school as most girls did
Played with Dolls and sometimes the boys
Would invite her to join them in pursuits
Away from Childish toys
But sadly Mum & Dad parted
As victims of Wartime spent apart
And for Polly this was a sad time to witness
Her Mum with a heavy and broken heart
But time passes now to her teenage years
Mountain climbing, motorbikes and Rock
For that was the Music she loved the best
Dressed in jeans or a long Hippy Frock
Then in the Village at Carnival time
When Polly was Deputy Carnival Queen

And her heart was quickly stolen
By a Member of the Army Motor Bike Team
They bided their time till the Army he left
And in 3 years the happy couple were wed
As Hubby left the Army and became
An ordinary civilian instead.

For a while they rode the Triumph together
Enjoying the thrill of the ride
But then along came the children
So motorcycling was put to one side
They were Oh! so proud of their 2 boys
Remembering the happy moments they'd had
Then up and left, as most boys do
And joined the Army just like their Dad
They had their share of pets in the house
Samoyed, Shelties & Poodles too
Along with a couple of Persian Cats
Which gave Polly plenty to do
In pointed hat she rode on a broom
Or dressed as an Indian Squaw
She always looked on the Wild Side of Life
To her that's what living is for
But life always has a downside
Pauline lost Hubby after 48 years
But with Sons by her side and determination
She slowly overcame the tears
And then as tho' a blast from the past
A letter from Aussie came
Written by a young Australian lady
Who told her their Dad was one and the same
After all these years she's found a Sister
Apparently a Brother in Scotland too
And brought back an interest into her life
Helping to pull her through
There is one thing left to mention

Polly's Internet Daughter Jeanne
Who's always teasing her "Witchy Mum"
As only good Daughters can
So now there is but one more thing to do
Before bringing this tale to an end
To wish Pauline health and happiness
With an Ode to an Internet Friend.

1st September 2008

Sandra the Sailor's Daughter

I'm casting back in my mind
And thinking for a while
And I really can't remember
Of and Ode about an Isle
So I think well that's alright
Why not try the Isle of Wight
That's a little plot of land across the sea
Now every Mum & Dad
If they really tell the truth
Will jump and shout for joy
If they have a little boy
But this Mum was in a whirl
When she found she had a baby girl
And Sandra was the name by which she's known
She may have gone to Ryde
For a game of seek and Hide
Or even gone to Cowes for yachting week
If that had been the case
Altho' it's being base
She could have there played hide and seek
To leave the Isle was tough
And the wavy seas looked rough
Every minute our Sandra looking paler
And some may sympathise
Some even think it strange
Cos' she's the daughter of a sea-loving Sailor
So from the Isle upon the Ferry
She sailed across the sea
To find out what her life would forfill
So when she finally got to Portsmouth
She jumped aboard a bus
For a ride just up the road to Selsey Bill
To me it's always been a mystery
Why Sandra studied History

Was it Captain Cook or Admiral Nelson or Francis Drake
When she might have been doing housework
Grooming her darling cats
Or even in the kitchen making a cake
Now she's never been a shirker
But has been a voluntary worker
Carrying out work of all kinds
Psychology is her inbuilt love
A subject so complex
Trying to study other peoples minds
So to end our little piece of verse
I think I'll take a chance
I'll put on some Latin American Music
And invite our Sandra to dance.

5th April 2008

SWEET LORRAINE

Now Stuart was a National Serviceman
At Shoebury Barracks with the Royal Artillery
He met and courted a Scottish Lassie
Jean from Greenock serving with the WRAC
Demobbed they both returned to Rotherham
Settled down and then they were wed
But couldn't settle to "Civvie" life
And rejoined the REME instead
For this is where they were happy
In uniform again
So this was an early start in Military life
For their little daughter Lorraine
Jean & Stuart had another child, I'm told
Though a little later on
I'm not quite sure exactly when
But I do know his name was John
Military Service runs in the Family
For this was plain to see
Grandad was a Gordon Highlander
A Scottish Piper was he
Schooling involved an event, it is said
At Manorbier and singing it entails
Where a little girls voice went Oh! so deep
When singing the National Anthem of Wales
They travelled the World together
As Dad was posted here & there
Whether it was out to Kenya or Germany
 Or sometimes a U K posting, tho' rare
Then after finishing school at Woking
On a Military Career Lorraine was so keen
That she donned the uniform of the WRAC
In serving the Country, Flag and the Queen
As a Pay Clerk at RPO Brighton
8 months in Northern Ireland as well

She's certainly "a chip of her Family block"
And that's not too hard to tell
Then it was off to Dusseldorf in Germany
Where she met a "Red Cap" with the SIB
And it wasn't too long before Lori and Steve wed
Which delighted the Family.

Their first born was a lovely young girl
And with joy they named her Claire
And the next year they were blessed with David
As company for their daughter that seemed fair
1990 and retired from the Forces
Back to the U K they came
And settled down quietly in Cambridgeshire
And found civilian life quite tame
They now have 3 dogs Cocker Spaniels
And Lorraine is Brown Owl in the Guides
Which she has done for over 20years
And housekeeping for Steve besides
Each Summer it means going to camp
Archery, climbing and abseiling too
As well as Status Quo, Abba with Dancing Queen
There's really so much to do
The Children now have a life of their own
Claire a Doctor, Paediatrician, is she
While David runs a Health Club/ Golf Course, in Australia
A fitness fanatic is he
But Lorraine and Steve as proud parents
Are pleased to see their children achieve
Their chosen roles in Society
And a Military Tradition to leave
I know that Lorraine still works in the Office
Of a certain Railway Company
But I expect that each day at 5
She dashes home to get Steve his Tea

The start of an Ode is quite easy
The Finale sometimes harder to find
Health and Happiness to you and your Family
From "Shrubby the Essex Bard" undersigned.

Dennis Shrubshall 19th November 2008

CAROL'S PRIDE

Elizabeth is a lovely name
But she was always called Betty for short
Which made things easier for Norman
In Germany where they started to court
Both together in Military life
With Betty in the WRAC
Norman was an Army Service Corps man
Then in the Army Ordnance Corps went he
The happy couple came home to London
In 1954 that's where they were wed
Returning once more to Germany
But as Mr. & Mrs instead
Continuing with their Service Life
Then in 1955
They were blessed with their first daughter Carol
Making Betty the happiest woman alive
Life was then spent as a Family
But it wasn't too long before
Along came little sister Linda, in 1957
Making this happy Family to four
They spent their lives as Soldiers families do
Travelling from pillar to post
To Hong Kong, Gibraltar, Germany and Wales
tho' not sure which they liked the most
Schooling became a problem
Which is fairly easy to see
For they never settled in one place to long
But they still managed to learn their A B C
The World was truly their Oyster then
But children don't realise
The importance of where they are living
But remember the Sea,Sun & Sand and Blue skies
So back once again to the United Kingdom
To Didcot in Oxfordshire I believe

Where Carol continued her schooling
Until it was time to leave
So now it was time to make up here mind
And a Military Career she chose
She donned the uniform of the QARANC
Service Life in her blood I suppose
In Rinteln in Germany she met and she married
A Soldier from the RAMC
Both working in Nursing.

For the welfare of the Miltary
And while they were at Rinteln their 2 sons were born
In the Military Hospital where they were employed
And once again two happy parents
Obviously overjoyed
Then they returned to the U K again
To Aldershot in Hampshire to live
And this was where their lovely daughter was born
Yet more parental happiness to give
When her 5 years service came to an end
And a few more years in between
It was back to Didcot in Oxfordshire
A Rural country scene
But sometimes life has it pitfalls
And a single Mum Carol became
She carried on like most single women do
And brought up her children just the same
As a Carer in the local Community
She's worked for over 20 years
And Branch Secretary at the Royal British Legion
Selling Poppies and some tales she hears
Of Battles past of our Soldiers old
And perhaps some that her Dear Dad Norman had told
But 10 years ago sadly her Dad passed away

To her he was always her best mate
And still he's been her Guardian Angel
Since that day in 1998.
But with Mum and the children give her the strength
To carry on along life's rocky way
And as we come to the end of this Ode
There's not much more left to say
So may I now in conclusion, say Carol
When you find that Life seems too hard
May I wish you all Health and Happiness
From " Shrubby the Essex Bard".

20th November 2008

ALL "WHITE" FOR CAROL

It was during the time of National Service
In the Pioneer Corps was he
Based with his Regiment in Cyprus
And thinking of Matrimony
Tho' twice the date was postponed
And eventually home the lad flew
To carry out his daunting task
He knew just what he had to do
Marriages are made in heaven they say
And this must have been Heaven sent
'Cos Norma the Bride & Brian the Groom
Got married in Burton upon Trent
At the tender young age of eighteen
When most young couples still courted
This pair of lovers made up their minds
They'd wed and get their life sorted
Unfortunately on their Honeymoon
Brian with Appendicitis was struck
They must have both thought to themselves
How can a couple have such bad luck
Three years in the Army was our newly wed
Then to Burton on Trent he returned
Now he was a civilian again
Another trade he learned
Then on one day in 1961
On the day of the Annual Goose Fair
Norma gave birth to a little Daughter
Her Carol with lovely blond hair
And later on a sister Susan
They were quite a lovable pair
Their Grandad was a jovial man
But had a peculiar habit
When they went to look at the Guinea Pigs
They found Grandad had eaten their pet rabbit

A few years on and they went to Stafford Street Infants
And then to Goodman Street Junior School too
Finally to Wolfric Senior where
There were more interesting things to do
Singing and playing Clarinet in the Orchestra
This young lady used to love it
Memories to stay with her all her life
Something to really covet.

When she left school to look for a career
 She spent some time in the Kitchen as Cook
And during the time she was doing this
For a Pen-Pal she did look
Who was Simon and he was an Army man
A 'fore long they were wed
Carol left her job in the Kitchen
And cooked for her Hubby instead
Later she worked at Catterick in the Laundry
The best job that she ever had
And with regret Happy Couple decide to part
Which is always very sad
But it happens in affairs of the heart
She'd lived in Bunde, Bielefield & Aldershot too
And again she decided to marry
Another young Uniformed Soldier
Whose name just happened to be Gary
Together they had two lovely children
The joy of their lives I believe
One of them named Thomas or Tom for short
And the other one Steven or Steve
But fate was to deal another bad hand for Carol in 2006
Bringing drastic change to her life
For her everloving Husband No 2
Ran off with his best friends wife
With Mum & Dad now in Argentina
And the company of young Steve and Tom

Nirvana, Guns & Roses, Robbie Williams & Take That
Is where her music is coming from
She now has a life as a Lady alone
And works each day in Reception
At the local Doctor's daily Surgery
To forget her tales of deception
By others in whom she'd placed her trust
How nice if the winds of change blew fair
And a Knight in Shining Armour might just
Ride off into the Sunset with Carol in his care
For I know that it is customary
For a love story to have a Happy end
So good health and happiness to you and your Lads
From"Shrubby" your Internet Friend.

27th November 2008

Part Four

More of Life's Tapestries

*A continuing display of yet more words in rhyme,
recording events of varying subjects*

MOTHER

Who was there to hear my first cry
When into this world I was born
To bring to my Mother the gift of love
On a Winters day 'fore dawn

She cherished me like a Mother should
And fed me and made sure I was warm
Then washed me and suitably clothed me
Taking care that I came to no harm

With 4 brothers and a sister to join me
A happy Family we became
All proud of this lady our Mother
With love she treated us all the same

When War came so did her worries
To feed us all was a chore
Mother would often have nothing to eat
So that we could have just that little food more

But love was there in abundance
And it grew with us through Life
Although to us this lovely lady was our Mother
To our Dad she was his loving Wife

To try to repay the love that she's shown
We all loved her in return like no other
For we were her loving Family
And she was always our Darling Mother.

9th March 2001

First Love

Can you sit in the chair and just ponder
When the first love of your life you met
It is probably something you cherish
A memory you'll never forget
When you met as the park gates were closing
And the Sunset was there in the West
Then you walked hand in hand
In your own Wonderland
Was your new boyfriend really impressed
Did the perfume you were using affect him
Was it maybe Chanel No. 5
And was he a real snappy dresser
Or perhaps about to contrive
The reason he liked your acquaintance
Your hair and the way that you dressed
Was it your smile and personality
Were they the things that he liked the best
Your next date was likely the Cinema
With two seats in the rear stalls
Only to find the Film breaking down
And the whole place was full of Catcalls
But you'd both spent the evening together
Young love in its first bloom
And at home was it bliss
When you shared your first kiss
As Mum & Dad left the room

But those days are now far behind you
As you sit alone in your chair
Was that first love your one and only beau
Or the start of a lifelong affair
So now as you look to the mirror
Have your Blonde locks turned Silver or grey?
Do you walk with a stoop, do your shoulders droop?
Or are you striding upright each day?
Is that first love still there beside you?
A lifelong romance in every way.

22nd August 2007

WHERE IS THE LOVE

Where is the love that once you knew
As it blossomed in your youth
The moon shone clear
And the Sun beams were bright
But did this disguise the truth
About how life can really be
As on life's road you travel
Tho' it make take so many years
The answers to unravel
For as you start upon the road
In dreams you still believe
How the Handsome Prince may come along
No thought that he might deceive
'Cos in those Fairy Tales you read
They have a Happy Ending
But love between a young couple
May soon see a cloud descending
When you sat in the room and your eyes first met
Was your heart all a'flutter and miss a beat
Did you ever think for one moment
It would end in lies and deceit
Oh yes, there were times you could jump for joy
And think of the happy times ahead
But alas sometimes things will go wrong
So you're there in the doldrums instead

Good times you'll always remember
Like the time you held your first child
You probably wept like the baby yourself
Completely and utterly beguiled
Which gave you the strength in those early days
To discover what life has in store
And should misfortune overtake you
You'll quickly show it the door
For then it will be time to open your heart
And seek in pastures new
To find love and compassion that you seek
Which may last the rest of life through.

28th October 2007

EGO TRIPPER

I've read your latest posting
And the words I must applaud
For you and I just write the words
Without going overboard
We write the words upon the page
Although from time to time
When browsing through them once again
May find that they don't rhyme
For sometimes things you want to say
The words your mind they elude
And then you're tempted to make them up
Or write in verse, a little bit cheeky or rude
If you recall I wrote the Shopping Spree
In fun in order to fill the gap
'Cos you said a poetess would be nice
I wrote as a lady not a chap
But if you feel I'm on an ego trip
You couldn't be further from right
As the last piece that I wrote, as a courtesy
To a lady member who liked what I write
I never demean but always praise
Another's attempts to achieve
Especially if they're writing poems
Their anxiety to relieve
So they too may fill with confidence
And write with vim and vigour
And that rhymes off the cuff will thrive
With an even bigger viewing figure.

OLD FLAMES

Have you ever looked back in your Memory
In the hope that you might recall
Those Halcyon days of the past
When stories of love would enthrall
Even without true intention
The thought of a very first kiss
Or a sign of recognition
Would not be considered amiss
Did you wave assent across the room
Or merely a nod of the head
Was there a hint of a warm caress
Did you turn your head away instead
Was there hope in your heart from the very first glance
Were you drifting away on a cloud
Or was this to be the one in your life
Should you shout out the name really loud
But no matter which way you turn it seems
That your newborn hope just shatters
For someone, somewhere will fill your dreams
And this is so clearly what matters
Remember that Kiss
And the warm caress
Or maybe a parting wave
As you go on through life
With your head in a whirl
Hoping your first love to save
And perhaps to re-kindle the flame that was lost
All those days, weeks & years long ago
Was that your name that was whispered just now
From the love that was lost
Or a new friend called to say Hello.

30th September 2007

SHALL I..? CAN I..? ANOTHER TIME

I sat at the table
With notebook and pen
I'm thinking of writing a poem again
My mind is in motion
But what shall I write
Of a ship on the ocean
Or gulls in full flight
The Opera or Ballet
On the opening night
Shall I look out at the moon in the sky
Even watch as a giant Jumbo files by
Will I wait till tomorrow
For the Postman to ring
To see what assortment of letters he'll bring
Some of them welcome
The others I'll hate
My eyes follow the Mail man down to the gate
It's raining again and I'm getting depressed
So I think it's time to give writing a rest
I've closed the book, put my pen on the table
That poem I'll write just as soon as I'm able.

The Emigrant

The boy stood at the door of the 'plane
His parents waved farewell
How long had he gone from their lives
Nobody could even tell
Say "Au Revoir" and not Goodbye
For parting is such sweet sorrow
Today he's gone but bound to return
In years to come or tomorrow
He'll come back again
With a smile on his face
Then throw out his arms
In a fond embrace
To a friend or relation he's anxious to meet
There's always someone keen to greet
The boy back home who should never have left
To travel across the Globe
To foreign parts and places unknown
Away from the U.K. he's all alone
The World's his oyster to probe
He'll try his hand at any task
He's ever so keen to succeed
True happiness is all he'll ask
In a world of financial greed
He tried the world of the outback
The felling of trees and lumber
Then back to the City he's changed his vocation
And taken some work as a Plumber
Rough work does not really suit
Such a man as himself
So he changed to being a Salesman
Selling off goods from the shelf
With the Ladies he seems to find
That he has quite a flair
They must like his well spoken accent or manner

Or the way that he shows them he'll care
But back now to working
Is not very kind
He'd sooner be "shirking"
With girls on his mind
At one time he tried driving buses
Worked in an Office as a Clerk
He shifted from Town to City
But never quite made his mark
Everything that he ever tried
He'd really given his "all"
But it never seemed to amount
To a fortune in his wallet
Or a staggering Bank Account
To Adelaide, Perth and Brisbane
He tried them all in turn
He worked and lived and enjoyed himself
Though never had money to burn
The streets were not paved with gold
As he'd often been led to believe
For only the money for which he worked hard
Was all that he'd receive
Over the years he saved a few pounds
For when fed up with wanting to roam
He'd pack his bags and board a 'plane
Back to H.O.M.E. home.

ODE TO THE WEDDING OF WENDY & PETER

It all began in '61
The story of Wendy and Pete
For their Mum & Dad
Were ever so glad
At the patter of tiny feet
But over the years
With their hopes and fears
Their paths seemed never to cross
Till luck took a hand
Waved a magical wand
And they both met at 18 Plus
Their glances were fleeting
But this fortunate meeting
Although it seemed destined by chance
For Wendy and Pete, this once weekly treat
had finally come to Romance
After a year when Pete conquered his fear
He asked Wendy's Dad for her hand
Take her Head and her legs and everything else
And finally the wedding was planned
Now Alfred and Bridget
They both sit and fidget
And Terry and Dennis enough said
As they sit in the pew
With nothing to do
But watch Wendy and Peter get Wed

Now to come near conclusion
Without fear of confusion
Our Best Wishes we're going to offer
To Wendy and Peter
We're all glad he did meet her
And we know that their Marriage will prosper
We know very well, that their future will tell
Of a Happy and Prosperous Life
Of Peter the PERFECT HUSBAND
And Wendy the PERFECT WIFE.

14th August 1982

LOST LOVE

As you sit in your chair and close your eyes
Your mind wanders to things that have passed
But Memories and Love are there forever
Throughout your life they will last
No one can know what is there in your heart
For you and one other alone
Your union was eternal
Which means you'll never be on your own.

March 2007

Passage of time

As I sit in my chair and close my eyes
But it matters not how hard I try
I do my best to visualise
The years are trying to pass me by
In the early years, when times were hard
When our worries were Oh! so small
We'd always find time to play in the yard
And wait for Mother's dinner time call
And as we grew older, long trousers in sight
For shorts we'd started to outgrow
And to bath in front of the fire on Friday, in private
Even when you were last in the row
'cos to Mother our bath night, was ever a chore
Hot water a thing we had not
'til a fire was ignited beneath laundry tub, full of water
To get twenty five gallons hot.
During the week at school we would study
And wait for the weekend to come
To play football and get disgustingly muddy
And come home to "an earful" from Mum
Before going to school on a weekday
A newspaper round had to be done
At weekends we went to work with the milkman
Delivering 700 pints on the run
And in the mid teens, when school was long past
A career not a hard thing to find
But deciding which type of job was best suited you
Went round and round in your mind
Then off to work each day of the week
Working from nine until five
To bring home two pounds, six shillings and fourpence
To keep body and soul alive.

The next step you took was a big one
Two years with the Flag and The Queen
Mandatory National Service
'tho young men never seemed too keen
A Uniform to wear with pride
And webbing and "blanco" and rifle
With a wage of a mere 24 shillings a week
At the time it seemed very trifle
Two years of your life you would never forget
The experience and friends that you'd made
I think it's time to bring this tale to an end
Lest my memory starts to fade.

16th February 2007

Dog Patrol

I've just picked up Shadow from the dog pound
He's more like a friend to me
Seems to know my every move and thought
He's like one of my Family
It's 22.00hrs on Friday
A weekend duty once again
And there are lots of things I could be doing
Than driving down this lane
Which meanders for miles on end it seems
From the City to the country beyond
It's our turn to monitor the industrial site
And a venue of which I'm not too fond
As it seems that the area is like a magnet
To all the low-life around
So while the site is closed for a couple of days
Criminals seem to abound
We've arrived at our destination
My friend Shadow and me
He's out of the van and makes for the first tree
And now that he's "comfy" he returns to my side
And on with his leash and with comfort he'll guide
Our footsteps in safety as together we stride
From building to building, ever aware
That a sneak thief or armed robber may be lurking there
As the corner we turn a lone car I see
Parked in a spot where I know it shouldn,t be
The headlights flash twice
And it flashes through my mind
It's a signal to a villain
Are they in front or behind
And Shadow has sensed my feel of unease
He strains at his leash
As though from his collar to squeeze
His heckles are up and raring to go

And find this intruder
Now his training will show
I've phoned for back-up in case things get bad
And hope above hope that it's only a lad
Or a couple of tearaways taking a chance
Of some easy pickings their drug habits to enhance
So we quicken our pace as a glass breaking sound
That would awaken the dead or anyone around
At the rear of a building a broken window we found
Had someone gained entry, my heart starts to pound
In the flashlight I saw bloodstains
So they were cut as they tried
Are they inside now or have they run off to hide
So I issued a challenge and let Shadow free
He dashed off in the darkness
Closely followed by me
As we dashed up the staircase
To the first floor, was there a second or third
How many more
Half way up the flight I heard a car engine roar
To a halt outside the building and the slam of a door
I ran down the stairs and heard someone shout
"There's a Guard with a Dog let's get the Hell out"
And the car sped away as I came through the door
And old friend Shadow returned to me once more.
The back –up arrived but once again too late
Which happens quite frequently
But perhaps we'd foiled a Burglary, Me and my mate,
That's what a faithful Guard dog can be
He maybe a Shadow by nature and name
But he's a very good friend to me.

9th February 2008

ARTISTIC TEMPERAMENT

I read your verse with thought so deep
And in my mind I try to keep
An image of a gentle soul
Who carries her maternal role
'Tho fate to her has been unkind
Yet still she carries on refined
To beat the demons lurking there
And even in moments of despair
Remembering loving moments past
Still to the future her mind will cast
To Talents regained in Acrylic and oil
She carries on her daily toil
And thanks the lucky Stars above
To regain an un-requited Love.

Having a Ball

The Stage is set, the time is right
We're gonna have a ball tonight
They're gathered here like they used to be
Just like a happy family
Musicians all ready to play
Many of the tunes of yesterday
Swing and Rock, New Orleans Jazz
They all really love the Razamataz
Casual dress, no suits or ties
Each one ready to melodise
They're ready to play and the audience hush
As the Pianists fingers across the keyboard rush
Drums are going to a steady beat
Everybody's started tapping their feet
 Clarinets & Saxophones joining now
Trumpeter too as he wipes his brow
Trombone's joined the happy throng
Double Bass steadily strumming along
They're really swinging this happy band
Even playing Dixieland
Traditional Jazz for the connoisseur
Hear those notes which sound so pure
Magic to the ears of the delighted throng
Happy to dance or just sing along
The lads carry on and play with ease
For it's not only the audience they have to please
But to satisfy their musical lust
In the knowledge they still enjoy & trust
That it will be many a year
Before they too must
Just sit back and listen, in their eye a small tear
While another generation plays the music
Traditional Jazz of yesteryear.

7th October 2008

Just Musing

As I sit alone in the early morn
Everything peaceful, the World still asleep
My mind often wanders to things that are past
For the hands of Time keep moving so fast
But they can't move the Memories I keep.
Of the times when a lad in the garden,
The trees then a pleasure to climb
When a penny bought sweets
And a trip to the Beach
Was a luxury every time.
once I went to the shops with a Shilling
A marvel it seems to relate
The purchase I made at the Co op
Made a suitable Dinner for eight.
New clothes weren't things that came often
And a Suit was for Sundays alone
A strong pair of Boots were for weekdays
For Shoes I was lucky to own.
Years pass and I work in an Office
As a Junior Clerk I'm employed
I even learned to Dance
Had my First Romance, my life till then I'd enjoyed.
I've drunk a few Beers
And just spent two years
In the service of H.M. the Queen
Wearing Uniform and Boots
Instead of nice suits
I saw places I'd never seen
I really turned out quite lucky
As an Airman they tried me, to teach
The mysterious wonders of Radar,
But I spent all my time on the Beach.
Came the time for my Service to finish
My thoughts at that time had to turn

What was I to do as a Civilian
Which Profession was I going to learn
To go back to the Railway I couldn't
New territory I'd have to invade
To serve in a Shop
I just couldn't stop
So I settled for the Building Trade.
I started work as a Chippy
And finally met my good Spouse
I used all my skills and before many years
I managed to build my own house.
The Children came along
First one and then two
Our House gradually filled with laughter
Hopefully me and my Wife, for the rest of our life
Living happily everafter.

ILLUSION

Looking into the shimmering water
Images many I can see
Is this just an illusion
Laying waiting just for me
What is the interpretation
Grey & Brown & Green & Gold
Orange too and there's some Silver
Surely these colours must unfold
Innermost thoughts of souls in torment
Happiness perhaps for some
What can be gleaned from this colourful Aura
Can the mystery be overcome
I think therein there lies a message
Maybe deep within the mind
Flotsum floating ever onward
Past the Diver returning with his find
When tinted oil is spilled upon the water
How will the vibrant shades all cope
Will they all intermingle
To form a giant Kaleidoscope
Was this all perhaps a Nightmare
On a bed as you reclined
Or was it all imagination
In an ever busy mind

31st August 2008

HORIZON

I look through the viewer
And what can be seen
Peace and tranquility
In the countryside serene
Flow gently Sweet Afton
Or so the poem goes
As the river seen here
So gently flows
Like the path of life
Till it disappears
Into the distance over the years
But still in the foreground
The trees stand so strong
As tho' watching the water amble along
Amid the reeds there sits a man with a wish
Perhaps today he'll be catching some fish
Is it the past or the future I see
On the horizon waiting for me
The houses so welcome
Somewhere to rest
After walking the countryside
The place I love best
To stroll through the meadows
Hear the song of a bird
Perhaps glimpse some cattle
Or horses preferred
As onward I amble
To the sunset I find
At a backward glance
The scenic beauty left behind

27th August 2008

Motorway Madness

Miles of concrete three lanes wide
Spreadeagled right across
The British countryside
Mile after mile of cars in a row
Where are they going no-one seems to know
Articulated Lorries and vans by the score
One or two drivers breaking the Law
Staring through the screen
Ever awaiting the chance
To display all their illegal skills
As from lane to lane they dance
Joined now and then by Motor Cyclists
As in and out they weave
In order to get to the front of the queue
But what do they ever achieve
They save a few minutes on a journey
At speeds sometimes horrific
Creating for some an early untimely death
To become yesterday's statistic
Now add to this some rain or snow
And conditions really get worse
With dirt and grime on the windscreen
Causing many a driver to curse
When over-taken by a Lorry
Perhaps whose mud flaps are missing that day
Creating a drivers nightmare
Being covered by a tumultuous spray
Evening now and streetlights are on
Albeit only here and there
Another excellent reason
For driving with the utmost care
But still there are the reckless ones
Without any thought or compunction
Who drive along like a Demon from Hell

'till they reach their specified Junction
Then they cross three lanes
Putting others at risk
To join the slip road very late
What is the need for their hurry
It is hard to speculate
To the ordinary discerning driver
Driving on the inside lane
Merely using the time it takes
To drive home safely again
They are pleased to return to the Urban roads
Tho' they view reckless driving with sadness
With a sigh of relief as they walk indoors
Away from the Motorway Madness.

24th October 2008

MY JAKE OF 16 SUMMERS

It doesn't seem that long ago
When we both first saw Jake
A little Jack Russell puppy
Which to our home we'd take
He did the things that puppies do
Even wee'd upon the floor
And after a couple of warnings
He didn't do that no more
He'd play out in the Garden
Or even welcome a walk
But he became impetuous
If we dared to stop and talk
He's been our friend for 16 years
Alongside little Nettle
Our other tiny canine friend
Who's really in fine fettle
But just like us they're growing old
And Jake is past his prime
And as his health is failing
He's in his Basket a lot of the time
To us they're more than a couple of dogs
And on us their life depends
Our Memories will be Eternal
Of our Little Canine Friends.

4th August 2007

Newly Wed

As a Bride she was a pretty girl
Oh! such a lovely sight
With Wedding Dress and train as well
Her body festooned in White
But when it came to time for bed
In "nightie" and long white drawers
Because she knew it only too well
Her Bridegroom perpetually snores
So in order to survive the Honeymoon
Without this couple coming to blows
She decided to end it there and then
And placed a peg on the end of his nose
Which cured the problem right away
But in the morning to allay suspicion
She'd remove the peg and look so serene
As a caring Wife with Tea and biscuits
Would be the Bridegroom's waking scene
Then as she bent to serve his Tea
Planted on his lips a kiss
Unaware of what had happened
Matrimonial Bliss
She now had set a precedent
Thinking her actions were right
But of course she's have to do the same again
Each and every night
With a smile or maybe just a few tears
For all the rest of her Married life
Perhaps another fifty years.

1st August 2008

ODE TO AN HERNIA

A year of waiting had come to an end
At the Day Care Centre, my stomach to mend
I'm met at Reception, and announce my arrival
Ever hopeful of this day's survival
'Midst hope and fears that are running rife
Will I survive the Surgeon's knife
But fears are allayed as Toni takes my hand
And ushers me round the "New" Day Care land
She shows me a cubicle, bed and gown
Then Toni for a specimen begs
Devoid of clothes I feel such a clown
And just stare at my knobbly legs
Maureen's here now, book and pen at the ready
Her stool and her instrument too
To check my age, my weight and B P
Have I had Jaundice or Typhoid or Flu
Now just as I'm musing will they operate by "Keyhole"
Or even the prospect of "Laser"
I'm brought back to earth by Maureen, who says
"Up with your gown whilst wielding a Razor
Now "Doc" has arrived and with friendly manner
Tells me just what to expect
Then on stomach, with marker pen, draws a circle and arrows
So the Surgeon knows where to dissect
Anaesthetist checks that I'm healthy, puts a tick by my name
'cos in the Day Care Centre, whether you're poor or you're healthy
Everyone's treated the same
So it's off to the Theatre with Toni by my side
And helped to be for inoculation
But strangely there are no worries to hide
I'm unconscious without a drifting sensation
It's soon over and I'm conscious, my mouth is so dry
Can my Dentures now be returned
Mouth rinsed by Recovery Nurse, a gleam in her eye

Today I've leant how Nurses wages are earned
Toni's returned now with Ken, I think
I can hear their friendly banter
To take me back to the Ward, on a trolley this time
And perhaps break into a canter
Deprived all day of nourishment
Or even a refreshing drink
Now we've Tea & Sandwiches served by Louise
Ably assisted by Pat I think
My treatment is finished and night time descends
I leave and say "Thank you"
To my Day Care Centre Friends.

Dedicated to Southend Hospital
August 1996

When you come home again to Wales

To look across the hillside
As far as the eyes can see
Only the Mountains and Valleys
In sheer tranquility
Some of the peaks with snow atop
Seen from the valleys below
This is where scenic beauty lies
As all the tourists know
For Wales has long been noted
As the Land of Music and Song
Where you can go to sleep
Just counting real Sheep
Seen in the countryside all day long
For far away a voice is calling
Peels of memory chime
Come home again come home again
It said through the echoes of time
To welcome home Welsh patriots
To the mining villages past
And look if you will at the buildings
Still covered in a film of coal dust
To explore some of the Welsh history
But to gloss over would be unjust
Picture the scene in the early morn
As the Colliers walk through the village for their shift
There's even a hint of a song in the air
As their laden spirits they try to lift
And take those last few steps to the pithead
Can you imagine how they might feel
Gathered together once more in the hoist
As the tired cogs start to squeal
And lower these heroes to the bowels of the earth
Not knowing what they might find
To hack and pick and shovel coal

Leaving their wives and families behind
While they work in the damp and the darkness
Even ponies were blinkered there
And each one loved by the pitmen
They treated their favourites with care
It's hard to imagine the life that they lived.

Below ground for all those hours
Hoping each day that aloft they'd return
To the welcome daylight and showers
But day after day, year on year
All some managed to achieve
Was to earn just a miserly pittance
And find it an effort to breathe
As older they grew but wouldn't give in
For they knew mining was in their blood
Their very existence relied on coal
Which they clearly understood
But sadly today the winches no long turn
To raise and lower the cage
As Coal Mining recedes into History
As a relic of a bygone age
And we go forward to a modern era
That Health & Safety would not condone
The un-healthly working environment
That Welsh Miners had always known
For many a Family the wrench was hard
Without Coal they had to adjust
And try to find other employment
To put food on the table, a must
I'm not too sure, for a Celt I am not
So it would have to be a pure guess
Not having to go down the pit again
Might have been worth just a little bit less

As long as body and soul were kept intact
For wives no longer necessary
To fear the sound of the siren, for an accident
Would it be their loved one,s they'd bury
I trust as this story is read now and then
Like other old Welsh tales
You remember the words of that famous song
"When you come home again to Wales.

8th August 2008

BIRDS

In the Winter, trees are bare
Robins we can easily see
Frost is always in the air
The Redbreasts hopping from tree to tree
Ever vigilant they move about
Moving from grass to branch
Hoping someone's thrown out food
Their hunger perhaps to staunch
To find some food it is a must
For our little feathered friends
Unwanted crumbs, perhaps a crust
They're glad when Winter Ends.
In the tree there hangs a stand
To fill with scraps finds and such
For the constant flow of little Birds
Who need the food so much
The delicacy they all appreciate
Blue Tit, Sparrow and Wren
I've watched through the window, as they sit and wait
For a refill of nuts once again.
They've eaten their trill
As I watch ever hopeful that I
In this cold Season, for whatever reason
A Greenfinch might identify.
Snow in the trees and thick on the ground
And the food although already sparse
Was impossible to be found.
From nowhere's appeared a half loaf of Bread
Round which Starlings are beginning to prance
Small birds in the branches start avalanches
In their eagerness to be fed
Spring's come with a rush
And there's a Hen Thrush
Selecting a site for her nest

Where day after day, on her eggs she will lay
Making sure none she will crush.
They hatch from their shells, this hungry brood
Ever waiting for Mother supplying their food
But as they have grown and their wings start to sprout
They've kicked their hard working Mother out.

Summer now and the Larks all sing
Warmth the Summer birds will bring
House Martins arriving with the Swallow
In mud and puddle she loves to wallow
With mud she fills her beak and leaves
To build her nest beneath the eaves, of the nearest House from
which she'll dive
For food to keep her chicks alive
Always in anticipation
They'll fly with her to Winter migration.

Life's Deck of Cards.

Life is like a pack of cards
No one knows what fate has in store
And I believe it is the gamblers in life
Who will play for evermore
Whether they win or lose won't matter
They'll do their best to win
Ever hopeful that their luck will change
Where others a coin will spin
Every player is eager
To see what a hand they've been dealt
Fate can be a cruel dealer
Downfall for many has spelt
Played as a game of light relief
Patience is the one people choose
A game played by one player
Tho' still you can win or lose
But much the same is the game of Life
When the stakes are running high
Opportunities grow and blossom
But bad hands fade and die
In the game of Life when you're handed and Ace
Or maybe Aces two or three
This raises your hopes of achievement
Arousing your expectancy
Of a change in fortunes inside your Family
To put you on the upward grade
Overcoming your difficulties
And bad times seem to fade
And it's now that you should play your Joker
Your opponents are now at your feet
As you stroll away from Life's Gambling Table
As a winner with happiness complete.

13th November 2008

MY ACCOUNT OF THE BELLS OF SANDERLINGS

I called at No. 2 Sanderlings
And pressed the bell that never rings
I knocked at the knocker that wasn't there
In an effort to make the lady hear

My reason for calling was to enquire
What shape or size she wanted her Fire
"I'm not quite sure " was what she said
It really depends upon my Edd"

When the Fire was done and I was going
They said "there's lots more jobs that we want doing"
The Porch to paint, the Step to tile
That concrete step looked really vile

Now they're looking less dismayed
The Pergola's built and the Patio's laid
Dwarf wall built and flowers planted
The garden's looking quite enchanted.

Have you finished now said EDD
I'm tired of getting out of bed
On Saturday mornings to open the door
Toe let you in for one more chore

To bring this tale to a conclusion
Before it conjures up confusion
I'll mend the bell that never rings
To please all the BELLS OF SANDERLINGS.

PLEASLEY

I'm driving down from Sheffield
Looking for somewhere to stay
And by the time I've got to Chesterfield
I thought I'd lost my way
There must be somewhere near here
A little village away from the crowd
Where I can sit and reflect on life
Even think my thoughts out loud
I see there's a sign for Scarsdale
Which brings to my mind collieries and pits
And the sight of the colliers finishing their shift
Through the dust on their faces, eyes are slits
I'm still driving on past Bramley and Glapwell
And Rowthorne is there on my right
Then as I pass New Houghton
Behold Pleasley comes into sight
Now I've never been to this village before
But I feel that I know it so well
The Black Boy, Swan, Pleasley Plough, Mason's Arms
All good drinkers pubs I can tell
So I made up my mind this is where I would stay
And booked B & B for the night
Then decided to have a wander around
And in the morning I just might
Take a look at the church of St Michael
Then take in St. Barnabus too
Have a quick look round the gravestones for history
As most nosey visitors do
But it's time to be on the move again
Mansfield's not too far away
So I'll bid farewell to Pleasley
Where I once spent an interesting day.

11th July 2007

PONDERANCE

I think it's always nice
To spend a few moments of one's time
To come on to a Website
And read or write some words in rhyme
The subject really doesn't matter
'Cos it's just a bit of fun
And helps to raise a smile or two
Bring happiness to someone
Who otherwise may sit and wonder
What a miserable place in which we live
It's only just some words in rhyme
And not a lot to give
Perhaps to somebody less fortunate
Who has to live alone or even in care
Whose wants and needs are minimal
But has love and compassion to share
For motivation is a must in life
In good health or even poor
And nice to welcome a smiling face
As you open your front door
So whilst you write your words next
Think of peace and tranquility
And the lives of the less fortunate
Instead of thee goes he.

10th September 2007

164

OH HOW I WISH I WAS FAMOUS

Oh! How I wish I was famous
For example like Adam & Eve
I'll bet Adam felt glib
Making Eve from his rib
But I find this a bit hard to believe.

Oh! How I wish I was famous

Like Shakespeare was with his writing
Instead of his quill
I wonder if our "Will"
Would have found a typewriter exciting

Now everyone knows
Of King Henry VIII
 Our sovereign was really astute
But was he after Nell Gwynn's company
Or was he really after her fruit

Did Admiral Nelson feel famous
Before he met his final demise
Laying sprawled on the deck
Did Hardy give him a "peck"
On the "Victory" 'neath the blue skies.

Do you think Kitchener wanted to be famous
Or was he a trifle barmy
As he brushed his moustache
Stuck his right finger out
And said "Britain needs you in its Army".

When Edison Bell was trying
A thoughtful experiment
Do you think he was trying to be famous
Or was the Telephone
Not his real intent.

Do you think Logie Baird
Had reason to be scared
Or had cause for great indecision
Did he really know that he'd be famous
When he invented Television.

... to be cont'd

ONLY ONE DALMATION

Pets may come and pets may go
But Memories live forever
Dumb animals is what they are called
But in fact they are very clever
They know and sense your every move
Even know the time of day
'cos they're always there at your front door
When you return to your home each day
They sense when you are happy
And also when you're sad
When the dog sees you pick their lead up
They are really glad
As they know it's time for walkies
In the Park perhaps for a game
But if it's only a stroll round the block at night
They enjoy it just the same
There was a time when a decision you made
That pets in the house were things of the past
But when Sonny Boy John came home with a puppy
Your mind you changed quite fast
For Pongo was full of Black & White spots
As all Dalmations are
He'd run round the garden at the speed of light
He'd beat animals near and far
But nothing was safe from this playful Pup
The Grand children he'd entertain
They'd stroke him and love him and brush him
Then do it all over again
And when he had finished his antics
And laid down I sighed with relief
Then he got up again and raced round & round
Even chewed up my false teeth
But sadly the years passed, he's no longer a Pup
And it's very painful to see

That our faithful Pongo is growing old
And I say in all humility
For 14 years he's been a friend and a playmate
For all the Family and me
And his parting came as a terrible wrench
With such finality
But I suppose if I was honest
Some happiness should be evident
That Pongo the Dalmation entered our Lives
Perhaps he was Heaven sent.

16th August 2008

PITTER PATTER

As I turned my head from a Sun kissed Sky
Would the weather today stay this way
Or is the Barometer falling
Will we have rain back once more today
I glanced again across the room
As the Silver clouds go scudding by
Acting like a shutter to the Golden rays
The blue has disappeared from the Sky
And looking at the window
Droplets of rain a pattern they form
Is this a passing shower
Or start of a Summer storm
And a pitter patter melody plays
Beating upon the window pane
It might be even prudent to call it
The Rhythm of the Falling rain
But then as tho' by magic
It went as quick as it came
Leaving a Rainbow in it's wake
Is there a crock of Gold to claim
Now I'll cease my watch on the window
Until another day's here
When I'll look at the weather forecast
And check if the Barometer reads clear.

16th October 2008

EMPTY PICTURE FRAME

I'm walking round a Studio
My eyes are full aware
To see the paintings on the wall
For there are many there
The paintings they are varied
The scenes that they portray
Depicted by the Artist
In many a different way
Some in Pastel, some with oil
In frames that glitter like gold
Each with a different story
Waiting to be told
Is the sky quite right I ask myself
Or the Moon upon the lake
Is the house in the right perspective
As a few more steps I take
I'm facing now to the Chimney breast
And as I stand and stare
I wonder why the wall is blank
'cept an empty frame hanging there
The Artist's now beside me
My curiosity's plain
Can you put into words an Ode she asks
To an EMPTY PICTURE FRAME.

The 'awkins of Rayleigh

'Twas in the year of '76
When I was in a dreadful fix
For without a decent "Sparks"
I simply couldn't carry on
The suddenly right out of the Blue
He said "don't worry 'cos I'm the one"
There came out little you know who
Mrs Hawkins favourite little son
David Hawkins was his name
And from Rayleigh in Essex he came
Along with his darling Wife Chris
She was a gem, or so he said
'cos when he used to munch
Her lovely home packed lunch
He found that she's put BUTTER on his bread
Now children they had three
But these I'd yet to see
At his home I'd never had a chance to call
Elaine and Donna were the girls
But they never had nice curls
For they were on the head of brother Paul
So a poem I said I'd write
On the phone the other night
About the Hawkins Family and me
So as this verse it ends
I'm very pleased to say
The 'awkins family and me are best of friends.

2nd December 1991.

POETIC LICENCE

Hi Colleagues it's nice to read your words
That you write from time to time
And even more especially
Because you write in rhyme
It really is a pity
That others we can't enthuse
To join the thread in unison
Should they ever feel the muse
To sit and write some words of verse
For others to enjoy
For it matters not the subject
Or the method they employ
Should they see a passing Elephant
Or a hopping Kangaroo
Or even a local Aborigine
Playing his didgeridoo
Is that a Eucalyptus tree
And a friendly Koala Bear
'Cos they're all likely subjects
You can mention if you care
For they're things you see in Aussie
But if you're here in he U.K
You could write of the rain or the floods perhaps
Or yesterday's Sunny day
Then there's cattle and sheep
And people asleep watching a game of Cricket
Or kids in the park playing football
To see just how far they can kick it
You can ramble on for hours
But I think it is now the time
To write the last conclusive words
And bring to an end this rhyme

7th August 2007

SUNDAYS

The dawn has come, the days beginning
Quickly Night will disappear,
Morning chorus of birds singing
Welcoming the Day break.
Will today bring something different,
Are my thoughts of things anew
The air is as clear as crystal
Now I feel the Morning Dew.
Is it April or September
Leaves of green or gold will tell
Calendar's not necessary
Signs of Nature show me well.
As I walk across the meadow
In the distance my eyes are gazing,
Where the mist just forms a curtain
To my side the cattle grazing.
On my ramble I continue
Now I have a stile to cross
Rustic timbers set at angles
Covered here and there in moss.
Ambling through the grass I notice
Here and there a rabbit run
Mushrooms sprouting, there's some clover,
Come's the rising Sun.
Mist is clearing, Blue sky's showing,
Senses bright, slight breeze is blowing.
From nearby lane there comes a clatter
of riders on Horseback the silence to shatter
Only the tops of the hats I can see
And hear their jovial chatter.
Moving onwards to the river
Ever hopeful I might spy
Kingfishers diving to the river
Or the ever present Dragonfly

There's an Angler, Umbrella spread
Rod firmly in his grip
Will I break his concentration
Will the fish give him the slip
As the river it meanders
On its never ending way
Tracks I make towards the road
Passing by a load of Hay
Coming down the lane a Tractor
Belching forth it's Diesel roar
Followed by an ancient Trailer, discarded many times before
Don't you think it's a pity when such a ramble ends
That you'll have to wait another week to meet Mother Nature's Friends.

Ruins on the Moor

The moor looked so desolate
Uninviting to me
But this was the challenge
I would face with impunity
To walk the path that very few trod
Looking for conquests new
Was there some danger lurking there
Beyond the Horizon so blue
The Sun was rising there in the East
A golden halo spreading fast
Tho' I knew that during my day long trek
This beautiful weather might not last
Mile after mile I strode along
Hoping directions were right
To study the ancient ruins
And get back to my lodging by night
All of a sudden came into view
A sight which to me was so rare
This wonderful relic of a bygone age
Gracefully standing there
And as I approached this ageing fortress
Or perhaps an Abbey of days gone by
And there through the crumbling masonry
Some portals I did espy
Or were they the remains that surrounded
The exit or entry therein
This was the start of my challenge
Where my adventure would begin
The trees drew themselves in a mantle
As tho' to shelter this magical scene
For grass had replaced the floors of stone
Creating tranquility serene
Curiosity has descended
Upon my furrowed brow

Shall I stay and see this scene by night
Or shall I leave right now
But it would be such a pity to go
For the dusk was Oh! so near
Would this be a treat in the moonlight
Minute sounds so very clear.

A couple of Rabbits go scurrying by
The last of the song birds sing
As I look to what may have been a belfry
Will I hear those ancient bells ring
The strangest thoughts all come to mind
As I stroll there all alone
Will I see the ghosts of a thousand years
As their fates they all bemoan
The time is passing quickly
Was that an old hinge I heard squeak
Will I see a ghostly hooded figure walk by
And in some bygone language speak
The Moon is full in the Heavens now
In a perfectly cloudless sky
Like a spotlight on this Crumbling ruin
Can I imagine if I try
To think of this monument in infancy
With horsemen riding by
Perhaps knights in shining armour
And damsels in distress as well
Apparently this is how it happened then
Or that is how I've heard folks tell
The dawn is coming up now
And I'm happy that I stayed
To see the ruins in different aspects
Ancient memories displayed.

So it's time for me to leave now
And make the return journey back home
walking across that desolate moor
Going home alone
When I could write a journal
On this fascinating day
A journey back to yesteryear
Perfect in every way.

16th September 2008

THE STEWARDESS

Every morning at nine fifty eight
She's there to open up the gate
Cos that's the job she has to do
I'll bet you're gonna ask me who
It's R E B E C C A.

She walks in through the double doors
To start her many daily chores
The shelves with beer she has to fill
And then she's got to check the till
Liaise with Secretary Bill
Who? R E B E C C A.

She opens the Bar, unlocks the Grills
Customers she serves and glasses fills
Packets of Crisps, biscuits and cheese
With her soft Scots brogue she aims to please
Some Members smile the others just tease
Their R E B E C C A.

At 11 p.m. she knows too well
It's time to ring the final bell
The Club will empty, she locks the Grills
Turns out the lights, empties the Tills
She's last to leave and it's very late
Because she's got to lock the gate
Who?? Dear R E B E C C A.

MA WEE SCOTTISH LASS

Ahm nae the man I used tae be
A figure so big and strong
As the years have taken their toll it seems
For the years just rush along
Across the hill and thro' the heather
Was ne'er a problem tae me
In Sunshine Rain and mist as well
For the Lassie I were going tae see
Alas Ah cannae walk that way again
My legs they are too weak
For me tae meet that wee Scottish lass
As that's the inspiration I seek
Can she nae cross those bonnie Scottish hills
Tae meet in my aen humble home
Where once again the flame of love rekindles
As we sit in ma house alone
And talk of the things of life in the past
And slowly reminisce
Of times in the mountains
Or down by the Lochs
Perhaps remember our very first Kiss
Scenic beauty Oh! so rare
Sunset on the Mull of Kintyre
On a typical wintry Scottish day
And then indoors tae a welcoming fire
Wi shared a dram as the day come tae an end
It's a toast tae you ma fair Lassie
Ma aen wee Scottish friend.

6th June 2008

THE CAMPBELLS ARE COMING –

Now as the story starts
It's the joining of two hearts
And Mr & Mrs Campbell they became
Devoted to each other
This lovely Scottish couple
Proud to have a Tartan in their name
Colin was the Husband
Elizabeth his charming bride
In Scotland they started married life
But nae the Mountains Lochs and heather
With it wet and windy weather
But on the coast at Kirkaldy, in Fife
In 1948 with the Midwife at the gate
In February first son Alan was born
They loved him like no other
And very soon produced a brother
David on a 1950 September morn'
Did they anticipate
That in March 1958
Their third son Colin would appear
'cos when you work it out
I don't think there's any doubt
Alan will be ten years old that year
Another seven years had passed
And a girl was born at last
And like her Mum, Elisabeth she became
For the boys a little sister
Mum & Dad could not resist her
Four children to carry on the family name
But childhood seem to quickly pass
The schooldays filled with laughter and tears
They all did the things children do
Before their teenage years
Elizabeth's dolls were set aside

Her friends were other boys
And the lads all took up Rugby
Discarded their Meccano sets and toys
Now David was seeking to make a new life in 1970
And leave the Family Scene
Enrolled in the Royal Army Medical Corps
In the Service of the Queen.

And there he served for 22 years
No doubt broke a few young ladies hearts
Even represented Scotland & Hong Kong
In the manly game of Darts
A sportsman it's plain to see
When David came home to the U K
He was even a Rugby referee
With his wife of 21 years now
Across the World they would roam
Living in and out of suitcases
With an Ambulance nearly his home
In a city in Saudi Arabia
Far from the U K shore
And after that they moved to Germany
Travelling the globe once more
Commuting to the Sahara
A dedicated Medic once more
But the time will come when enough is enough
And once more back to their native land
To witness the thrill of the Highlands and Lochs
Away from Arabian and Sahara sand
And visit Mum and the Family
'tho sadly Dad is no longer there
To retire to a life as a civilian
After a lifetime of Nursing and Care
To live the life of a Pensioner

And listen to Abba or Queen perhaps Blake
Read a detective novel in the Garden
As on the Sun Lounger you flake
And your Wife emerges with cold drinks
On this lovely sunny morn
What about putting that book away
And get up and mow the lawn.

Exit stage left. Ha ha!

24th July 2008

DREAMING

As daylight ends
And night descends
The time is drawing nigh
For counting sheep
And go to sleep
In slumber perchance to dream
But once we've closed our eyes it seems
Not knowing the reason why
We climb a Mountain
May swim a lake
Or sometimes even fly
We walk through beauteous gardens
Wander through woods and by streams
And even fight the devil himself
When terror rules our dreams
The night goes fast
With thoughts of the past
Of the things that might have been
A game in the park
Or a kiss in the dark
But it's only just a dream,
Do we rule our destiny
Forever working and scheming
Or is the answer we really seek
Relaxing and simply DREAMING.

September 1994

Spring In View

In the bleak of Winter
At the window I stand and stare
To see which of Nature's wonders
Withstands the Arctic air
A silver blanket covers the grass
Frost glistens in the tree
But here and there in little bunches
Daffodils I see
The Crocus and the Snowdrop
And even Jonquils too
Join the fading Winter Jasmine
Indicating Spring is surely due
Regal Camellia blooms are lying
'midst leaves with silken sheen
Majestic Magnolia blossoms opening
Flowering Cherry will soon be seen
Hyacinth and Polyanthus
Side by side in beds
Surrounded by colourful Violas
With pretty variegated heads
Weather's warmer, Sun is up
Grass just grows and grows
Also Dandelion and Buttercup
Oh! look, Summer's very first Rose.

INSPIRATION

I feel a little guilty
With my pen I've had a rest
From putting words together
And rhyme them with the rest
I know that sometimes people read
The ditties that I write
And then I got to thinking
Is what I'm doing really right
Should Members really have to suffer
To scan these lines of text
Or is it really in their thoughts
"What will he write about next"
Adversity is my middle name
My motivation true
'cos I like writing Poems
When my working day is through.

West Bay

Strolling on the promenade
Quite early in the day
The view that I encountered
Was a turbulent West Bay
The clouds they rolled in Oh so fast
In varying shades from white to the grey of slate
The weather had altered drastically
Stormy and intemperate
The raging sea crashed against the shore
Throwing up a silvery spray
Reaching across the roadway
Drenching all who passed that way
Although pedestrians there were few
Who really found the need
On a day like this, to stand and stare
At the rocks all covered in seaweed,
And here and there was evidence
Of refuse from passing ships
Or perhaps from holiday makers
With discarded wrapping of Fish & Chips
But the sea it looked so angry
An uninviting Opal and grey
Tho' they say let's go down to the sea in ships
It's not a good choice today
So stroll on now to the hillside
To the rocks of white and green
Where the grass has found a place
To grow and create this beautiful scene
So as you leave the Sea behind you
On this cold and desolate day
You can sample the delights of Dorset's hillsides
And return another time to West Bay.

23th June 2008

THE SIMPLE LIFE

Whatever happened to the simple life
Where people were carefree and gay
Even the word at the end of the last line
You mustn't mention today
We live for political correctness
No inference should ever be used
As there might be misinterpretation
And cause persons to be confused
You've got to be very careful
With a colour scheme on your mind
'cos if black is one of your choices
Some opposition you might find
Be careful to add in some Yellow and white
When decorating a home that's palatial
And throw in some red & green & blue
Or someone might suggest that you're racial
Don't try to buy a Golliwog Doll
Or a Teddy bear try to name
As it might be misinterpreted in Arabic
And you'll be the one that takes the blame
You may walk in the street and be confronted
And feel on your handbag a tug
As you turn you may see a young hoodlum, in a "hoodie"
You're now the victim he's trying to mug
But you don't give in without fighting
With your fist you catch him full in the face
To the do-gooders you're now not the victim, but assailant
And the Police cart you off in disgrace
With young thug getting compensation
And then disappear without trace
So now if you will cast your mind back
To the times when you were but a mere Child
And Angels we certainly were not
Standards of behaviour were stringent

And wrongdoings were never forgot
Perhaps the fear of the Policeman's gauntlet
Or a swipe round the head with his Cape
Or his threat to tell all to your Father
Then you knew there was no escape
Even the criminal fraternity knew
That if knife or a gun they should use
The Law then was very specific
And they would die in the Hangman's Noose
So now as I sit and contemplate
And slowly close my eyes
Whatever happened to the simple life
I'll leave you all to visualise.

11th December 2007

STATUESQUE FOUNTAIN

Walking in the Stately Gardens
Relaxation was my aim
I wondered who on earth lived here
What was their claim to fame
Maybe they inherited it
But own it just the same
A leisurely walk in the afternoon
Enjoying the Summer air
And came across this Idyllic scene
Free of trouble and care
The centrepiece was a statuesque fountain
Streams of water rose high and wide
Surrounded by trees and reeds and foliage
As though the pool was trying to hide
But the sunbeams had managed to creep though the trees
Giving leaves a golden hue
Casting it's light on the water cascading
Creating a startling view
Now I have noticed the huge tree standing there
Like a guardian over this beautiful scene
And from it's size it clearly indicates
How many years this has been
A place of sanctuary for all to come
To enjoy tranquillity and peace serene
Before journeying on to further explore
What more of Natures wonders abound
Hidden here in the English countryside
Waiting to be found.

7th June 2008

WOODLAND WALK

A hike in the forest
On an Autumn Morn
It's an early start
As a new day is born
Everywhere damp
With the dew of the night
The air Oh! so crisp
What a glorious sight
Row upon row of trunks so erect
Climbing up to the sky
And most of the foliage nearer the top
Into which early birds fly
The ground is littered with twigs and bark
Listen to the songs of the Linnet and the Lark
Trudging through a carpet of moss and grass
Rabbits scurry to their burrows
As slowly we pass
Looking upwards and what do we see
What is beyond the furthermost tree
Brown & Green, Gold & Blue
Intermingled making a colourful hue
The Sun is trying it's hardest
To penetrate this vast wooded hollow
Giving hope to the hikers
As the well worn signs they follow
By those who have trodden this woodland path
To enjoy the pleasures of a casual walk
As they amble along so aimlessly
Interested in casual talk
About how to spend many happy hours
On their leisurely weekends
With an open ear and open eye
And meet some of Mother Nature's friends.

3rd October 2008

SAILOR'S CABARET

To think of you bouncing over the sea
Adrenalin running wild
With an ever eager excitement
As when you were a child
And having tried the boating scene
I know to you just what it means
The peace as the world just passes by
The Sun at it's peak in a cloudless sky
Whoops what's that Seagull dropped in your eye
Oh! dear It's lucky they say
But luckier still if they missed your head
And the deposit lands in the sea instead
The birds that follow in your wake
Hoping some scraps from you they'll take
Or into the ocean they may dive
Immerging with a fish they've
caught alive
Audaciously sit & devour 'pon your bow
And Whoops!!! that's all gone through them now
As they wing their way once fed
And you're alone with the wind and spray
Wondering what else you'll see today
Porpoise or Dolphin, or seals and Sharks
All getting up to their various larks
This is the Sailor's Cabaret.

29th October 2007

TWILIGHT

As the sun begins to fade
And the night is drawing nigh
Out of the window I set my gaze
To the slowly darkening sky
Which now has changed to a darkening Pink
That's edged with a ribbon of gold
It's a truly magnificent Sunset
A pleasure to behold
But as the day just slips away
The silence seems quite muted
Devoid of the myriads of birds
And songs liberally distributed
Amongst the hedgerows and the trees
Their joy was shown with singing
As freely they flew in their world in the sky
Or on some of the treetops clinging
Tho' now not a sign of a bird can be found
As the darkness of night closes in
Nocturnal animals on the ground
Their night-time scavenge to begin
I nearly forgot the wily old Barn Owl
Perched in the rafters since the morn'
Patiently awaiting the return of the fieldmice
On the floor, and eating the corn
Circling the chicken coops again
Was the fox on his nightly habit
Unless on his journey he might waylay
A poor unsuspecting rabbit.

After these few hours of darkness
Whilst most of the people sleep
The sky is getting lighter, it seems
As the watch of the dawn we keep
And if we care to stand and listen
If only for a minute
Perhaps we'll hear the chorus of dawn
The Blackbird, The Lark and The Linnet.

19th January 2007

STRESS

Life goes on from day today
We live our life the way we see
But always in the background
There but for him goes me
We think of things that might have been
But never came to much
And sometimes we will get irate
At even the smallest touch
Of a word that's said in anger
Infinitesimally small
Was there any need for an upset
Not any need at all
Tho' everyone's got troubles
Troubles by the score
Where once they never worried
Now we worry evermore
From time to time we suffer loss
Of someone we hold dear
And wonder are we strong enough
For all the pain to bear
But most folk are resilient
Their torment they can share
With a friend they know will listen
And also truly care
About the way they think and feel
When filled with deep emotion
Patience that is endless
As well as deep devotion
For now as I read the words I write
To some, may seem meaningless
I think I've found the answer I want
To cure the feeling of STRESS.

8th February 2007

VICTIM OF ALZHEIMER'S

Your plight is recognised Oh! so well
But Children do not fret
For she is still there, the Mum you knew
So do not get upset
She may not comprehend what you say
In another world she may live
But all the love she gave to you
Is still there for you to give
For as we reach the twilight years
For some it's not too kind
As all the lovely Memories
Become muddled in your mind
But patience is still a virtue
Even tho' at times a strain
Always ever hoping that things will come right again
The sympathy of others
Tho' little comfort or consolation
Is all that they can offer
As outsiders in the situation
I know from my experience
The tasks you have to face
To cover Oh! so many things
In such a little space
Of time which is always well filled
Multi tasking you do best
Which makes you so strong willed
And fit to face the test
So close your eyes and think awhile
Of the times and memories passed
And you'll realise why you must go on
For life is going so fast
And I'm sure in my heart as I have trodden
The road that you tread now
You'll find that super hidden strength

And you'll cope some how
For a Mum is something precious
As everyone will know
Whatever it takes you'll do it
And never let her go.

15th August 2008

SOPHISTICATED LADIES

It's years it seems
Since first we met
Exactly when I just forget
Upon the stage
These tiny mites
Rehearsing on Tuesday & Thursday nights
Ever alert they await the chance
For the year to come when they will dance
Ballet, twist and even Rock
For sweets I bring they thank me
Then 'don' their tights on 'Panto' nights
And dance their version of "Spank Me"
They've grown up now, no longer chancers
But lively entertaining dancers
Claire, Louise and Lindsay too
The girls that I know best
Are joined each year by other girls
With their dancing I'm impressed
Sophisticated Ladies, though young
Good friends for quite some time
And I'm their personal Poet
Their GRANDAD OF THE PANTOMIME.

*Written for a little girl 12 years of age suddenly diagnosed with
Leukaemia who was one of the dancers in the Pantomime.
Thankfully she recovered.
12th February 1995*

DOLL'S FOLLY.

Come follow the Band
To Pantomime Land
We'll see what make King Arthur tick
Dolly wants this Production really slick
Occasionally flares up so very quick
She's waving her hand.

Now listen to me
She say's to the cast
I just can't sit here watching this
Ian reckons you're all taking the "p..."
He shouts "No no" and shakes his fist
Just learn your words fast.

Well the weeks fly by and it's difficult to tell
If the cast will satisfy Producer Dolly Bell
Ian blasphemes in the middle of "Thou Swell"
"Bloody awful again"

The cast tries hard and it's very plain to see
They struggle with their words with great difficulty
But they're definitely better even Dolly will agree
Though not openly

Ian stands and he pleads and Heather's there as well
Will the Show be a success only time alone will tell
They're up on Stage and mis cue Camelot
Dolly shouts "No no, what a load of bloody rot"
Just follow the Band.

Dress rehearsal tonight
It should go with ease
The Stage is set, the music's really swell
The Opening's fine and dictions good as well
Ian & Dolly grin as they see the cast excel
They're in tune with the Band.

The Cast worked hard and the Stage crew too
To prove what Dolly really always knew
Everything works out on Opening Night
Like Lancelot's arrows in full flight

Let's follow the Band.

Written to the music of "Come follow the Band"
21st February 1995

LEVINGTON

In a lovely little village
In a County known so well
In the depth of quaint old Suffolk
Or so I've heard folk tell
There lived a loving couple
Mr & Mrs Arthur Wade
To see them walking hand in hand
What a beautiful sight they made
You could see them every Sunday
As they travelled down the lane
It's 10oclock and time for Chapel
To worship once again
Suitably dressed for the occasion
She'd wear best coat and hat
And gloves to match as well, I think
You could safely bet on that
And Arthur in suit and polished boots
A very smart man was he
'cos he sometimes donned the Uniform
Of the Special Constabulary
But on a certain Wednesday afternoon
Village women all assembled there
Outside their local Village Hall
Where they could only stand and stare
As a coach filled with strange young children, arrived
And from the coach they did alight.

Tired, frightened and dishevelled
They looked such a pitiful sight
As they filed into the building
They knew not what to expect
For they were here all alone
Without Parents to protect
Them for the first time it seemed

That they were on their own
But love and understanding
Was quickly to be shown
By the villagers of Levington
Who were ever eager to please
These youngsters from a wartime City of London
To be known as Evacuees
Their purpose here today, they knew
To give the children a temporary home
Away from the bombed and blasted city
And in peace this country village to roam
There were 30 or 40 Children on the floor
Waiting for the Ladies who, they, might pick
Although the likely lads did find a home
The pretty blue-eyed, fair haired girls went quick.

Five of us were left now
Three brothers, my Brother and me
But everyone chose single children
It seemed no-one wanted two or three
The three lads were adamant
Their Mum said they shouldn't part
When along came a Lady, with a house the boys would hold
Not only that she had a great big heart
And now I return to the start of this Ode
And the Memory I have will never fade
Of the Angels who were our Saviours
And live forever in our hearts
Mr & Mrs Arthur Wade
They treated us as though their own
This couple mild and meek
And all they got in financial help
Was a mere 10 shillings a week.

5th February 2007

A SAILOR'S FAREWELL

As I walked through the gates for the very last time
And heard them close behind
My eyes were closed by a flood of tears
As the thoughts seemed so refined
The memories, to me, came flooding back
Of happiness and sorrow
As I realized that what was past
Would not be there tomorrow
The furlough's and the binges
And the women we've loved at a cost
The battles in which we've taken part
And the colleagues that we've lost
Was I right to sign away my life
Not knowing what I could have had
But that was all so long ago
When I was but a mere lad
But the clock can never backward turn
And you're a "civvie" now
So pick up your bags and forward go
Wipe that worried look from your brow
It's time to plan your future
For fate can be unkind
You'll never forget your time in the Andrew
It's eternal on your mind.

15th April 2007

IS THE WORLD YOUR OYSTER

If you were given the choice
To live where you wish
In this great big World where we live
Would it be a hard decision to take
What considerations would you give
Maybe the Culture or Climate
Comes uppermost in your mind
Is it a sun-kissed solitary Island you seek
Where peace and seclusion you'll find
Perhaps far North in the Artic
In the land of a thousand nights
The Aurora Borealis
And spectacular Northern Lights
Or are you looking South from there
To the Ffiords in Norway maybe
With a nice little fisherman's cottage
A boat and fishing trips out to Sea
But it's cold very cold in these Northern climes
So further South we must go
Have you set your sights on Europe
In Holland or Belgium or France
In a nice little village you know
Past Spain and Portugal as onwards we sail
Past Gibralta to Mediterranean and Sun
We've travelled now a good many miles
Since our search for a Home was begun
Will it be Florence, Rome or Venice
Or the North African shore.

Or one of the little Greek Islands
Like Kos, Majorca, Minorca or more
I forgot about Sicily and Ibiza
Where holiday-makers go by the flock
But I'm sure if you chose one of these venues

You'd see how they all run amok
So onward we go and we're out of the Med
Down the West Coast of Africa, South
Avoiding Kenya for Capetown and Durban
Having seen the size of the Lion's mouth
When we watched the film about Safari
As we cruised in the waters Blue
For apart from eating and drinking
There was little else to do
We've changed our mind about South Africa
We're going to give Jo'burg a pass
As we sail across the Indian Ocean
Thank goodness we're travelling First Class
'cos the heat is nearly unbearable
As we are approaching Bombay
So we sail straight on past Singapore and Thailand
Until we reach Australia for a stay
We tried Perth & Adelaide & Queensland & Sydney
But we really weren't impressed, I must say
So we were back on ship and sailing again
Bound for the U S of A
Like the Pilgrim Fathers in the Mayflower so long ago
Those dedicated Quakers so plain
But when we docked in the East Coast in Miami
It was full of Holiday Makers... again.

And soon we left on our constant search
Only this time we went by train
The journey was long but the miles flew by
As through City and State we chased
I did try to make a note of them all
But somehow that note got misplaced
We finally arrived in the Big Apple
Which, I must say, lived up to it's name
For everything there is bigger and better
But that's the name of the game

It wasn't the place we'd like to live
Tho' we've travelled far and wide
We're crossing the Canadian Border
To the land of the Great Divide
And I must say the Canadian Mounted Police
In their Uniform of Scarlet and Blue
Stood out again the snow clad background
Forming a colourful hue
We saw Ontario, Ottawa and Toronto
With not much further North we could go
For all that was left was Alaska
Frozen wastes like the land of the Eskimo
It's so long ago since we left the Arctic
And circum-navigated the Globe, that's nice
To find there's not a lot here in Alaska
But lots of Snow, Snow Snow Snow & Ice.

26th December 2007

RESPONSE TO DEPRESSION

Try if you will to close your eyes
And think of memories past
The times when you had a smile on your face
As on happiness your eyes you cast
But then your life has gone through change
Over these many years
With strain and stress and tragedy
Accompanied by tears
But this is the way that you relieve
The pent up feelings inside
Reality you can't run away from
For there is no place to hide
But if you look to the future
At the end of the tunnel there is light
And the end of your depressive state
As everything turns out right
With the help of the friends you know
Who will help you along the way
If not in fact in deeds themselves
They know the right things to say
To guide you back to the bright side of life
With understanding and tolerance shown
These are the things that prove to you
You will never be on your own
And then you will go from strength to strength
And search and find fields anew
In fact the world is your Oyster
And it's waiting just for you.

27th August 2008

206

MEDITATION

It matters not what thoughts you have
Every one has the right
To close their eyes and meditate
On how their past just might
Have turned out Oh! so differently
From the life that they now live
Tho' sometimes terrible mistakes we make
And then ourselves forgive
But now and then it's nice
To give our feelings vent
And then return to reality
Perhaps more happy and content.

2007

MELODIOUS INTENT

So listen to the rhythm of the falling rain
And see if therein a message lies
For the gentle tip tap on the window pane
Which you can readily melodise
And add the words you want to hear
Come forth to you once again
And you have now created a Ballad
The Rhythm of the Falling Rain
For this is surely one method
Of how songs come to start
And depict our innermost feelings
Or matters of the heart
Wherein we may soar above the clouds
Or merely float on the crest of a wave
But sometimes wallow in a mire
Strange how our minds behave
Not really knowing which way to turn
For 'tis all written in the book of life
Experience is the way to learn
How we overcome trouble and strife
To identify your inner desires
To choose which path is right
Then you can sit at your friendly computer
And compose love songs all through the night.

20th January 2008

Brighton Launch "Voices of the Poppies"

I woke one Saturday morning
Not so many weeks ago
With the prospect of a drive to the South Coast
To a Book Launch we were to go
The journey we made without incident
Although the rain was ever present
Had we picked a sunny day
Most likely it would have been more pleasant
Brighton in Sussex our destination
Not knowing fully what to expect
At the venue at Jubilee Library
Perhaps meet a Lady of great respect
Finding a suitable place to park
As the rain kept falling down
Didn't enhance our prospects
In this very busy Sussex town
Bu luckily after a circuit or two or three
Of the streets I came to know so well
I found a spot right next to the Library
Luck was with me that day I could tell
So into the palacious building we entered
Not knowing what we would find
Climbed the stairs to the Conference Room
To find Helen the Publisher reclined
Well actually she jumped up to greet us
And make us both welcome there
And introduced us to other Forces Poetry guests
With whom the afternoon we'd share
Light refreshments were available
As we waited for the honoured guest to arrive
Who was none other than Dame Vera Lynn
And she too had to make the long drive
As Patron of "Voices of the Poppies"
With Remembrance on her mind

Ever knowing as the Forces Sweetheart
A lovelier Lady would be hard to find
Now the time for the performance to start
 Dame Vera with Mac the aisle walked down
Taking a seat beside Helen the Publisher
Who introduced this Lady of great renown
Then standing up Lady Vera spoke to those assembled
Words of wisdom and her purpose in life.

To entertain and give strength to the Military
She was the Forces Sweetheart in times of Strife
Some Members then read their chosen verses
The effect of which was not a surprise
As you cast a look at the audience, and Dame Vera
You'd have noticed the tears in their eyes
Giles Penfound had captured it all
In his famous trusty camera lens
And then it was back to the tables, for book signings
Eagerly offering Dame Vera their pens
In their books to capture the signature of this great Lady
That the whole of the United Kingdom adore
Then walk away with a smile on their face
And know it's in their book evermore
As a lad I remembered Vera. as she was then
A "Dollybird" and Forces Sweetheart too
And here we were 60 years later
And it is Lady Dame Vera I'm asking who
Would attempt today what she did then
To travel the world unaccompanied by ladies
To entertain Britain's fighting men
Not for a day or a week by the way
But month after month anyhow
Which prompted me then to say, Lady Vera
You're still the Forces Sweetheart now
She took time to speak to young and old
No "airs or graces " there to see

Just a likeable, lovable English Lady
Which to me she will always be
For me this was an afternoon to remember
As our aims we were able to achieve
To promote the sales of "Voices of the Poppies"
And hope some Veterans suffering to relieve
By the funds of a deserving Charity
From the revenue earned from sales of the book
And give the Forces Poetry Website
Perhaps an enthusiastic future to look
To create more publications
And poets more poems to write
In order to achieve their eventual aim
To give assistance to War victims plight.

23rd November 2008

ECBA LEICESTER

I've been up to Leicester
And drove home again
You've all guessed the answer
It did nothing but rain
For 130 miles it was dry
But down came the rain
And I felt I should try
To look on the bright side
Perhaps it won't last
But as I peered skywards
It seemed overcast
And then it came down
Like a funeral shroud
Until it finally emptied
That enormous raincloud
So the game was called off
To the Players dismay
A rematch impossible
So far away
Then we sat down to Tea
Of a salad and sweet
With cheese and biscuits after
The meal to complete
Then all the words spoken
By the President's two
With apologies for the weather
And thank players too
So the final occurence
To this eventful day
150 mile homewards
What can I say.

26th July 2007

HI DE HI TO G.I. JANE

Words are free to every one
Just take them one at a time
Then juggle them all about a bit
To get them all to rhyme
The subject doesn't matter
As long as the page you fill
You're doing it for achievement
It's not a special skill
You're trying to paint a picture
Using the written word
And when you look at the end results
You think well that's absurd
But if you've enjoyed the writing
For other folk to read
With plenty of enthusiasm
As a Poet you'll succeed.

Not William Shakespeare but Old Shrubby
August 2007

THE SHOPLIFTER

Since I was a "Special" some years ago
A story has stayed on my mind
When we were called to a shout, my mate and me
And wondered what we would find
The call came over the Radio
For the 2 of us to attend
At the local branch of M & S
A "Shoplifter" to apprehend
We were met outside the premises
By the "local" Constable there
But when introduced to the Store Detective
She gave us all such a scare
"Dragon Lady" came to mind
To describe this lady of large proportions
Just one dreadful stare from her
Had more effect than warnings or cautions
We entered the Store, then her Office
The alleged "Shoplifter" incarcerated there
And when we 3 Uniformed Officers entered
It gave the poor chap such a scare
As he sat on the chair by the table
While "Dragon Lady" her evidence gave
About how she'd followed the suspect
And watched the way he'd behave
And to prove her point , on the table she tipped
The bag and it's contents were emptied
And when I saw what was lying there
To laugh I was sorely tempted
There were Knickers and Bras and Pantyhose
Lingerie of every kind
Oh! how I'd like to own all that
Was what came rushing through my mind
And now with her daunting task finished
"Dragon Lady" gave us a request.

Would you Officers now do your duty
And this suspect you should arrest
"Yes Ma'am" was my colleague's speedy reply
As we took the suspect by the arm
We could tell from that worried look in his eye
That he wouldn't do us any harm
As I come to the end of this intriguing tale
There's but one thing I'd like to say
Don't get on the wrong side of the "Dragon Lady"
'cos with her, crime definitely doesn't pay.

28th December 2009

MIGHTIER THAN THE SWORD

It's nice to sit and ponder
About the things that people write
It helps to while away an hour or two
As you sit at home each night
For some just like to have a "chat"
Others like the Forums to read
Some subjects seem to get out of hand
Then an Arbiter they'll need
To consider all the "pro's nd con's"
And the evidence is scanned
Then issue an ultimatum
Before some folks understand
As Ron has said so eloquently
From his home so far abroad
Many have been slain with a Biro Pen
Much mightier than a sword
Now the reason I mostly write in verse
When I've a minute or two to spare
Is to avoid the general Forums
Which usually end in Political Warfare
I know that here in Rhymes off the Cuff
It's a fairly safe place to be
For knowledge and education
Perhaps some joviality
So as I pen these final words
As Sunday Evening descends
I trust that this Thread goes from strength to strength
For Ron and his Forces Reunited friends.

21st September 2008